KU-016-809

SWINDON COLLEGE

LEARNING RESOURCE CENTF

THE RED BOOK OF GROUPS

by

GAIE HOUSTON

CONTENTS

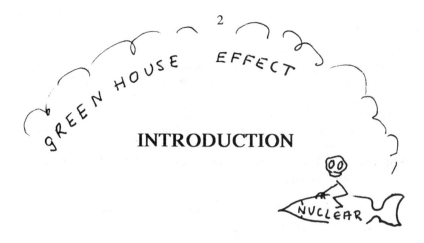

INTRODUCTION

At last, we are giving more attention to the fact that organisations are kept going not by Staff or Pay-roll, but by people. People need to feel respected and worthy of respect. They need to belong, to be in contact with each other, to feel competent, recognised, lovable and loving. And one of the ways of dealing with these holistic, these whole-person, needs, is to set up a small group. Its stated task may be support or social skills learning, or it may just be called the home or peer or growth, counselling or whatever group. Even study, research and supervision groups need often to be a good home for their members - not an ideal or idealised home, but one where there can be comfort and honesty, some love and some loyalty and the exchanging from time to time of home truths.

So far so good. Except that people need the group because they are short of time, or skills, or both, to do all their psychic housekeeping informally. As a culture we have been brought up to have bad feelings about bad feelings, and generally suppress them. We have gone through years of statutory schooling, being told what to think on which subjects at what moments, so our creativity is likely to have wilted a little. We have often been slyly trained to value people for their social status or wealth or cleverness, rather than their compassion or laughter or emotionality.

In other words, there is a slight touch of Falstaff's army about most of us when we first turn up at an interpersonal group.

For many of us, being direct with people, letting ourselves be straight, knowing what we are feeling, even listening, are much harder than we suppose. All of this makes leading such a group much more difficult than teaching people to dance or tie sheepshanks.

Many of the books I have read about small groups, are devoted mainly to describing some of what is likely to occur, in a diagnostic way. They give less space to suggesting how to cope with or change what is happening.

My hope is that this book will help you be more confident and skilled in leading, so that everyone in the group can become more effective, and enjoy themselves. I have set out to help you communicate accurately and clearly, to understand more of what may be going on between all of you in the group, and to suggest many exercises or other structures to empower all the members to take charge of their lives, in the group and elsewhere.

HORSES FOR COURSES

Most chapters of this book include some exercises you can do with the group. This one does not. It is a reflective piece for you, as leader or potential leader, to help you notice more how you lead, and what else you might try if your present style does not suit you, or you and the group. Finding your way of leading is not like choosing a hat, ramming it on your head and forgetting it. For example, however much you admire some gentle acceptant therapist you know, you cannot wear his style for long at a time if you are a lively, pushy, talkative, impulsive person. You will more likely be effective with a more initiative or didactic way of working, say psychodrama or behavioural counselling.

As well as inviting you to study and respect your own needs as you read this chapter, I give some space to describing some overt and covert ways of leading small interpersonal groups, which for many people seem to have thick cobwebs of mystery around them.

A band leader is not an impressive figure if the band refuses to play. On the other hand, babies can look to my eye most impressive leaders, when they get a whole posse of adults to coo and nod and play peep-bo with them. In other words, no-one can function well as a leader unless whoever is supposed to be led will join in. In other words, you need to get a response from your group, and be in reciprocity with the members, to be a leader at all.

This may, as you sit in the comfortable isolation of reading, seem so obvious as not to need being said. However, there are armies of trainers and consultants going about the world talking about Motivating the Staff, Motivating the Work Force, Motivating the Group. Most of this work looks to me a direct result of setting up groups and organisations, and admitting new members to them, in a cackhanded, literally a misleading, way.

Chapter 2 deals with ways of building in likely success in setting up a group. This one is about styles of leadership, and their possible effects, good and bad.

And I want it here
in this office in
20 minutes,
or you're fired!
Get it?

This can be called the Attila the Hun approach. It is at one end of a line which leads to the opposite, who might be called Rabbit.

I know you're frightfully busy,
but if you could manage, well,
just a draft of the September
figures? Say by Christmas?

Attila the Hun is likely to upset all but the most robust members in a ward-group, a committee, or most groups I can think of. But with Rabbit in charge, people will soon be frustrated that no decisions are made, no actions taken, that the group is not defended or disciplined or stimulated by the leader. It seems as if groups need to know and enforce some rules within the group, and to guard their boundaries. In other words, any group needs controls, and is likely to look to the leader to provide them.

I insist on some rules and structure

I'm the visionary

I think clearly

We want the leader to keep us together and help us use each other well.

I take care of us

I can get us moving

I'll bring out feelings

I know how other groups work

6

Another sort of leadership is to do with magic and love, to do with attractiveness and excitement. Charles Handy uses the Greek god Dionysus to illustrate an aspect of this sort of leadership, which often has love, and some eroticism and licence, around. Mae West is an earthy example of the same kind.

In its highest form this sort of leadership is inspirational, and fires people to hope, and to becoming the fullest expression of their powers. Christ is the archetype of this, apparently easily able to call people from their jobs and families, to live a life of material rigour, and spiritual fulfilment. Mao Tse Tung is a striking modern example of a leader who functioned strongly as a charismatic figure, as well as being decisive, and generally competent.

Perhaps Uriah Heep is a fair example of the opposite of all these inspirational qualities.

Think of yourself as group-leader. Imagine your physical pose.

Being competent is often singled out as one of the main ways of being a leader.

If a swarm of bees flew into the Cabinet room, then any passing bee-keeper would be likely to take command over all the august people there, since knowing how to gather the angry swarm would at that moment be the most valuable kind of competence present.

To you it may be clear that being clever at bee management is not alone enough to justify, say, immediately promoting the bee-keeper to be Prime Minister or Foreign Secretary. Yet, in a less dramatic way, something like this happens in many organisations and groups .

People who are very good at one of the craft skills of their industry, say selling, or broadcasting, are, because they are seen to have that competence, promoted to doing something else, which they may turn out to do poorly. If so, they tend to stay in that job.

An astute writer expressed this as the Peter (his name) Principle, of elevating everyone in an organisation to the level at which they are incompetent.

For some tasks, members of a group are perhaps justified in demanding competence from the leader. Teaching, or allowing-learning, is part of the work of many support or interpersonal or therapy groups. People are likely to come to the group with a clear expectation that the leader is more skilled than them or knows something they do not. They expect to have that real dependence on the leader, at least for a time. If they knew it all beforehand, they would not have needed to join the group.

For other tasks, it may not matter so much whether the leader is good at the central job of the group. Take our example of selling, or broadcasting, once more. Salesmen need to be trained, to be kept informed, and to be kept in touch and cheered up in a sometimes lonely task. Broadcasters need a very complicated back-up cf programming budgets, technical resources, and personal encouragement and monitoring, if they are to broadcast well. The person who can organise all this, and have a shrewd judgement about the moment to moment psychology of the broadcasters, does not necessarily need to be a wonderful commentator or presenter or actor himself.

Most groups which are primarily concerned with the psyches of their members need their leaders to function part-way between the two styles talked of here. Every human being is an applied psychologist.

Listen at any market stall or on any bus, and you are likely to hear personal, even idiosyncratic theories of motivation. You may or may not agree with these theories. That is beside the point. What I am suggesting is that we all reflect on why people do as they do. Then we come up with theories which influence our behaviour and seek to adapt to, or change, theirs. This is applied psychology.

So, the leader in this sort of small group is not teaching a brand-new topic, like sailing or computer literacy. She is to some extent negotiating her ideas of how people work, with the ideas of other group members on the same subject. And everyone present has, willy-nilly, spent a lifetime already in research. All of this can, and in time probably will be an asset to the group. But at the beginning it can also make the going rough.

FOUR CURRENT LEADERSHIP STYLES. IS THIS HOW YOU WANT TO DO IT?

WONDER-CHILD

If you have reasonable goodwill, want to be liked, and have had no training in working with groups, you have possibly tried out this style without quite meaning to. One sign of having done so is to find after the end of the session that you have a splitting headache, and a tendency to kick doors and scream.

This shows that you are not temperamentally suited to being a Wonder Child, who tries to be all things to all people, and has a vague notion that good leadership means taking on booking the hall, making the coffee, understanding poor Mrs Jackson, coping with little Sammy, having worthwhile opinions on all topics, chairing the meeting faultlessly, being everybody's therapist and doing the washing-up afterwards.

Wonder-Child models impossible perfection of a conventional female kind. She gives no space for the abilities of other people. Her slogan might be Nice For Everybody.

THE LOVING SHEPHERD

This animal smiles a very great deal, and on the face of it is like Wonder-Child. He radiates charisma, which often turns out not to be backed up with deeds to match the promise. Some of the more dubious religious leaders who abound at the moment are good examples of what I call Loving Shepherds. But there are numbers of lesser shepherds and shepherdesses tripping through the flowery meadows of most organisations.

They bask in warm feelings, make sure that any bad feelings are directed at somebody other than them, and manipulate their colleagues or others to carry much of their work-load. In a small group, the Loving Shepherd will use much of the time Sharing His Problems with the people he is being paid to work with.

I assume that you want to work in such a way that people in your group have a larger range of options than being centred on you. I hope too that you do want to release more of people's good feelings. The art is to notice if you are becoming a greedy feeder, wanting only love and praise. Then, if you want it to, this book can help you allow good and bad feelings roost where they belong, instead of being perched on a few people who turn into symbols of Good and Bad.

Both these styles flourish where there is not much training, and where there is very woolly supervision. They are largely self-taught. As well, I come across two adaptations of excellent orthodox styles into something I doubt to be of lasting use to the unfortunate group. These adaptations are common enough for me to comment on them here.

A large, respected and worthy school of small group work sees the staff member not as a leader, but as a consultant. Her task, which is rigourously supervised, is to try and interpret what members are doing, in terms of, for example, the unconscious forces in the group.

To do this, the consultant sits quiet much of the time. Sadly, many psychiatrists and others who have attended such groups, end up with the notion that if they sit in any small group in almost complete silence, they are leading it effectively. Certainly, they are having an effect - just by being there. They are probably annoying some people, depressing others, and causing the rest to use a good deal of psychic energy simply to deny their presence.

It is likely that most of you who read this book are working with groups of people who want to learn to approach each other with more trust. They do not need an apparently sadistic leader, who models distance and non-communication.

One of the positive aspects of this style is the reminder that silence can . on occasion be more effective intervention than ·constant leading from the front.

JUST ONE OF THE GROUP

One American orthodoxy in running small groups, is to have the leader painstakingly model full and honest communication, insofar as she is able. Near the start of the group, she might suggest some guide-lines for everyone, such as

listening fully
noticing your own responses and telling them
communicating accurately
noticing your feelings as well as your thoughts
talking directly to people
staying here and now.

Inevitably, the leader who follows this advice is very self-revealing, and does in many ways function as just one of the group. Unlike Idle Jack.

No wonder that many people who have been in both sorts of groups are smitten with the warmth and apparent easiness of this latter style. That seems fine. But some of these long-way-after followers have the firm idea that their job is only to bare their souls; it is not to lead, or, in the special jargon, it is to be non-directive.

At worst, Being Directive is seen in such groups as bad behaviour. How boring! If nobody ever tries to push anyone else around a little, the group may turn into a steamy compost heap of deep feelings and no action. Like being silent, refusing to take a lead can be an effective way to get other people off their butts. As an unvarying style, though, it is not necessarily all pure virtue.

So we come round again to the idea of horses for courses. You need to match the various ways you know of effectively being yourself, with the task and the personalities of the people you are working with. You are a member of a social species with strong tendencies to co-operative as well as competitive behaviour. Under whatever learned responses, whatever personal distress they are feeling, the other members of your group have the same capacity as you for understanding and generosity, wisdom and creativity. As long as you remember these facets of all of you, you are likely to free yourself to be the best of yourself as leader. That may for you mean being an orthodox this or that. It may mean using many different ideas and methods.

2. STARTING THE GROUP

People are cussed. Tell them that spinach is good for them, and that what is more you have cooked them some and they are to sit down and eat it; the chances are that few will comply, and fewer yet will enjoy the spinach, than if you had left them to work the whole spinach question for themselves.

So it is with groups. Get it into your head that your street, hospital, department, or education institution needs a small support group, find some funding, choose a room, and advertise, and you may have immense difficulty in recruiting or in keeping members. It is your group people are invited to, not their own.

In his book about Mao Tse Tung, "The Long March", Edgar Snow describes how he came to recognise that there would be a big meeting: people kept going in and out of each other's caves or tents, in ones and twos. That to me is an illustration of one good way of beginning any participative group. People have a series of hopeful exploratory conversations, which coalesce into the forming of a group. Everyone already knows at least one other person. Everyone has chosen to be there.

In Zen there is a tradition of the Whispered Transmission. One explanation of this is that people will listen if they want to hear. If you tell someone receptive about the advantages of a small group, and a little later have someone else ask you if you will join or run one, then the whispered transmission has worked. If you put out your message two or three times, and hear no more, then it is possible that nobody is interested, and you had better look elsewhere, or take up a different hobby.

Before you do any whispering, or any other kind of advertising, be sure that you know what the potential group is for. Begin your Long March with several conversations about this, with people you hope will enrich your thinking. If, for example, you are an occupational therapist in a psychiatric hospital, you might want an O.T.'s group to improve your skills at working with groups of patients. After talking, you might decide to ask doctors and nurses and P.S.W.'s into the group, too, if they are all doing the same task. If as the head of a department in an organisation you see the need for an informal group, you need again to talk over whether you want to recruit people in your own department, or some other people entirely, such as other heads of department. In a college group, do you want students and lecturers and administrative staff in the same group? In each case, you answer connects strongly to

WHAT THE GROUP IS FOR

Very many of you who read this book will work with groups which have been formed with minimal consultation with the people in them. In most education establishments, pupils are told what they are to learn, rather than asked what they need. In hospitals, much treatment, partly because of the special knowledge of doctors and nurses, feels to the patient like a power relationship in which they take the lesser role.

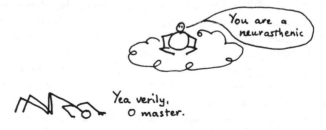

In very many businesses, the word consult is used freely, but nobody is really asked for their opinion at all.

At the other end of the scale is Carl Rogers' way of beginning counselling groups, school classes, any series of meetings in which full participation by the members is desirable. He apparently sits around and waits for someone else to begin. He believes, and states to the group, that they can make a far better job of deciding what they want to learn or achieve, than he can on their behalf. His task is to understand what they are saying, by listening to them and checking that he has the sense of their words. I stress that he actually explains these ideas to people, rather than sitting in baffling smug silence, as I have seen some other of his long-way-after followers doing. I have worked in Rogers' way in many settings, and like the results. After gossip, and hopeful looks at me to see if I am going to call order, the questions that slowly emerge are some form of

What are we here for?

What do we want to do?

How do we want to go about it?

At this stage there may be some excitement. There is even more likely to be a certain amount of bad feeling: the leader is not galloping on a white charger at the head of the column, but sitting around listening to everyone; time seems to be being wasted.

If your nerves are not up to this apparently formless beginning to a group, and the spats of surprise and disappointment that may be directed at you, you may like to use some structures to take care of your and everybody's anxieties. As well as giving a feeling of safety and purpose, such structures make it likely that everyone has a say.

First, let me stress that any exercise or structure will fulfil more than its overt purpose, as I have begun to hint in the last paragraph. And, as well as being useful, it is likely to have a few side-effects that you may notice later. One is that if you as leader keep producing them, the members will come to think that you always should. They will at worst become dependent and resentful, and you will be over-taxed and fractious, like the old woman who lived in a shoe. (I bet that if she had not assumed that she was the only person who could allocate resources and exert authority, the children would have shared the management of the household with her.)

If people have not met before, they will very likely want to be introduced. Most of us have been on the sort of short course which starts with announcements about mealtimes and how to get into the squash court, then proceeds to each person's being asked to say who she is, give a career resume and her principle reasons for being on the course at all. I have poor retention of what is said on these occasions, as I am usually nervous, dislike almost everyone in sight, and am mostly occupied with composing my own little speech.

However, if you want to reduce anxiety, that is one, albeit long winded, way to do it. People have time to study each other's faces and clothes and manner, as well as hear what they say, as all take their turn.

INTERVIEW

To give more participation, ask people to pair up, and then take turns interviewing each other for 3 minutes. Two pairs then meet, to make a foursome, and each person introduces his pair to the other:

This is Cyril from Central Services. He likes sailing....

This is Sally. She's got six salukis.

The fours then come back to the whole group, and each person makes a one-sentence introduction of one of the other pair in her foursome.

If people know each other already, or half-do, or are strangers who want a self-revealing group, this next exercise may suit, in one of the forms here, or another you invent.

SOMETHING SPECIAL

Ask people to say their names, and tell one thing pleasant or unpleasant, that has been in their thoughts a lot in the last few days.
Or. Ask them to say one thing they hope to change in their lives within the coming year.
Or, in a small group, ask them each to tell one idea about their own future they are playing with at the moment.
Or, ask them to tell one thing they are pleased with themselves for doing in the last 24 hours.
Or, ask them, maybe using a cushion or empty chair to represent themselves, to show their attitude to themselves just now.
Or, ask them simply to say their name and what they are feeling, and what image goes with the feeling.

As I say, I prefer the unstructured or jungle beginning, in which everyone has to hack their way through the dim undergrowth, if a clearing is to be made in which we can work. But these structured introductions seem useful where time is short, say on a one-day or half-day course, or where people seem so intensely scared that you want to reduce their anxiety.

TO TELL THE TRUTH

Becoming a member of a group is full of psychological peril. I may turn out to be unacceptable to the rest; (so I may guard myself against that by deciding that they are all unacceptable to me). I may not be recognised for my talents; so I may show off, or else clam up. I may find that the other members' assumptions about the group, about me, about life, are so different from mine that my view of the world will disintegrate; so I may want to take charge quickly, to bully my world view on to everyone else. The group may not seem the cocoon of goodness I sought.

In these and many other ways all group members have probably developed some fears and some ways of dealing with the fears, in response to the mere idea of the group they are to join. They have started working in the group, before even coming to the first meeting. It can make a fruitful beginning to let people focus on all this and talk about it, comparing the reality with the fantasy. After they have done so, you may need to ask about their hopes too, and how they can set about realising them in the group.

There is some scare around.

Where?

Well, generally.

In you?

Er yes.

How do you notice it?

I'm shaking from head to foot.

What are you likely to achieve in this sort of conversation? People may discover some commonality, in having the same kinds of dread. By talking about that dread, they will probably dispel or reduce it. So, at best, they will begin to move from a feeling of being unskilled or powerless, towards taking charge of themselves and what is to happen in the group. As well as this, they may have begun to learn to listen as fully as you are listening. You may have had a chance too to encourage them to be specific rather than general in what they recount.

At this stage of a group's life, I like to do some joint planning, more or less informally. A rule of thumb is that the more people there are in the group, the more formal you may need the planning to be, if everyone is to have a share in it. Here is a formal structure I have often used.

ENVISION

Ask everyone to shut their eyes for two minutes and remember what made them want to come to the group, and imagine what they want from it for themselves. Some people have great difficulty in knowing what they want. I am not of the transcendental cast of mind that yearns for the yogi way of being, beyond all earthly desires. I think such a way of being is socially, politically and psychologically suspect. So I encourage people to find out what they are wanting from moment to moment.

Next, ask them to write down a few key-words, to remind themselves of their thoughts and imaginings.

Then get them to pair, or make threes or fours, to talk about their expectations, and make a list on a large paper, maybe scored for popularity, of everyone's wants. Join in the exercise yourself. If there are enough staff to make your own sub-group, you may gain a lot from making a list together. The excitement and possible dissension that are often a feature of planning meetings will by this means be made clear to everyone, instead of being part of the staff mystery.

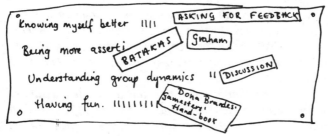

These lists are then put up on the wall and left for people to inspect, perhaps through a coffee-break.

Next, ask people to write how they would like to tackle all or any of the ideas on the lists. Ask them to write these hows, which are methods and resources, on small bits of paper, which they Blu-tack on to the wall-lists, after consultation in their small group.

*An advantage of the Blu-tack is that negotiations can stay clear.
For example, if Graham, who has offered to do an assertiveness
session, turns out to despise discussion as a way of understanding
group dynamics, he may want to volunteer a workshop on that
subject instead, while Sally takes over the assertiveness work.
By now it may feel right to get a sense of how much time and energy
people want to devote to each topic. One way is to ask them, once
more in the small groups which produced the lists, to make circle
diagrams, which they can then negotiate, or at least show each
other.*

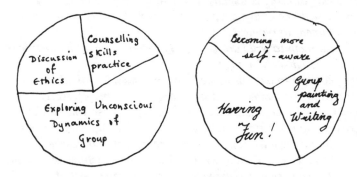

*If diagrams as different as this appear, there will be plenty for
people to talk through. The assertiveness training mentioned earlier
will be one of the issues that comes straight into view, whether in the
form of verbal combat, or more negatively, by people deferring to
each other and generally talking themselves out of what they
actually want.
It is quite likely that at about this time a few silent assumptions
have tip-toed into the group. One of them might be that if the
members decide on what they want to deal with, then you will see
that that happens. They may think of themselves rather as
restaurant patrons, who have made their choices, and now hand you,
the waiter, their orders. They are to sit back and be fed, or be
finicky, and you are to serve up the dishes.One way of hauling this
assumption out into the light of day is to ask how people intend to
see that their needs and preferences are catered for.*

When members turn appealing smiles on me at this stage, and tell me that they feel I shall know just what to do for the best, I resist this, quite tempting, invitation to be the all-wise benevolent guru, as gently or otherwise as i judge appropriate.

"You're putting a lot of trust in me. Are you saying I know what you want better than you do? I don't believe I do."

"So I know best for you? Do you make any limits to that? What don't I know best for you?"

"I don't want to take on being responsible for everyone getting what they want. It's hard enough for me to attend to what I want."

"One thing I want is to be effective. I don't believe I shall be if I'm trying to do everyone's work."

These are a few of the responses I might make. They show my way of working, which may not at all be yours. What I do see as effective is to speak economically, to pick up fast on what is happening, and to show my involvement in it, rather than just highlighting the other person's.

The next chapter is about some of the tasks I see the leader usefully taking on, and my ideas of how to go about them.

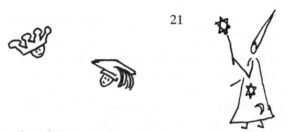

3. MAGIC, LEADERSHIP, DYNAMICS

Tribes have chiefs. Nations and states have monarchs or presidents. Navies have admirals. Hospitals have matrons. Many small groups have a leader. People have an undeniable tendency to single out one or two to be Top among them, and to set them up as prestigious. In a magical way, people often behave as if the worth of the leader is to do with their own worth, so that her or his prestige is that of the whole group.

Some thinkers say that when we create leaders, we are at least in part trying to re-create a mythical early childhood for ourselves, in which there are all-powerful, omniscient and adorable parents who will take care of all our needs and our troubles.

If that is so, them it certainly looks as if another aspect of early life comes in. Babies are reckoned to have many murderous fantasies, as well as the raging fury of the comparatively powerless that most parents have clearly witnessed. You may have observed that being a head of state carries a statistically large risk of assassination, deposition, banishment, imprisonment and other forms of early retirement. In other words, people clearly behave in a rather florid, larger than life, way, to leader-figures.

If, as I do, you accept that there is this element of irrationality around everyone's perceptions of leaders, you may decide that you had better at once set up a leaderless peer group. Or perhaps take up a solitary occupation like angling, and so avoid the whole question in a different way.

Setting up a leaderless group does not, in my experience, altogether deal with the issue. The old tendency creeps out of the wainscot, and we make a mostly unconscious attempt to turn someone in the group into the leader, because she's the prettiest, or because the meeting is at his house, or on some other interestingly nutty excuse. If this is noticed, and people take the opportunity of working out their own needs for, or needs to discard, what I am calling magical leaders, then much may be learnt.

What I have found more often in leaderless groups is that everyone is working so consciously and hard at the idea of being egalitarian, that they do not let themselves wade into this curious and informative swamp around magical leadership.

I saw this most clearly when I was a student on a student-centred diploma course, in which we had to make our own submissions to the academic board, decide our own syllabus and do much peer and self-evaluation. The whole experience was intensely educational, often in quite unlooked for ways. (Having a fellow-student become hypnotised into believing she was a crocodile, and getting stuck like it for a week, was a piece of traumatic learning it took some time to profit from, for example.)

However, we did not to my mind ever Work The Authority Issue, which is another way of saying, deal with our notions of magic around leadership. The staff on the course were certainly far from dictatorial or leaderish. In fact they were often not there at all. What I see as having happened is that all the students stayed in a good-children mode until almost the final moments of the course. Speaking for myself, I know that I took heart from thinking that being self-reliant, co-operative, inventive, and so on, would be approved of by the staff. So I was being apparently adult, from an approval-seeking motive. Only in the hideous, though therapeutic discomforts of diploma-awarding did I and others awake to confronting the staff. By then there was not time to do all that might profitably have been done.

What is needed, to my mind, is to make a winnowing of The Great Muddle Between You And Me, which I describe in The Red Book of Gestalt.

In this instance some of the muddle will perhaps show up in this table.

FALSE LOGIC OF THE INFANT-GROUP MEMBER
MARK I

MEMBER		LEADER
I feel dependent		*You are totally dependable*
I feel ignorant		*You know everything*
I feel powerless	*THEREFORE*	*You are omnipotent*
I need affection		*Only yours is good enough*
I need approval		*You must give it*

SMALL-PRINT CONTRACT

If you the leader, agree to all this, I will let all my good
feelings flow towards you, and I will suppress my own needs
to be leader.
If you do not come up to scratch in any of the above
particulars, I shall direct bad feelings at you until you choke,
run off, or beg for mercy.

As leader, you may find that you set up a complementary
set of assumptions, or double-binds, for yourself:
You feel dependent   *So*   *I shall be totally dependable.*
You need approval   *I shall disguise my disapproval.*
The Infant-Group Member, by which I simply mean
anyone at the beginning of the group's life, may produce a more
hostile set of conclusions, perhaps along these lines.

FALSE LOGIC MARK II

I feel dependent		*You must not know my weakness*
I feel ignorant		*You're ignorant too*
I feel powerless	*THEREFORE*	*I won't allow you any power*
I need affection		*I'll not spare you any*
I need approval		*I'll keep disapproving until I'm invincible.*

In saying all this, I am trying to describe the totality of
what is going on in people at the beginning of a group. I have been
in groups, indeed, where the issues of power and authority have
hardly been addressed, and yet much that was useful was done.

This book is about leadership, though, so that is why I am keeping on about it.

As leader, you have to make your own judgement about how far you will go along with people's expectations, and how far you will see' your work being to let them notice what those expectations are. I am not evangelical about making people break through to this or that enlightenment which I am already in possession of. I see it as preferable to work at what energises or is of interest to most people present, at the same time not suppressing my awareness of some of what is going on but is not at that moment being talked of.

Much of this chapter so far is about some of the feelings and expectations that may lurk partly out of awareness, and which are to do with unrealistic, even archaic, hopes and feelings, apparently towards you, but really towards your role, your magical position.

Alongside these, and usually tangled up with them, goes each person's adult judgement about the leader's fitness for the job. If I sign up for a group to learn assertiveness, and the leader is so embarrassed and deferential that she has difficulty even telling me to turn up on time, I can understand her interest in the subject of assertiveness, but may well doubt if she can teach me any skills in it. So my rejection of her will have some adult rationality. (The amount of feeling I have about her and her lack of skill, the extent to which I rage and blame at being betrayed or misled or whatever I choose to perceive, will probably have a good deal to do with my magical expectations, too.)

GOOD ENOUGH LEADERS

This exercise is a way in to finding everyone's feelings and expectations about leaders. Begin by a brain-storm. This is simply a minute or two during which everyone is invited to call out any words that occur to them in connection with the subject - in this case, leadership. You or someone else, maybe two people if the group is large, write the words as they are called, on a blackboard or flip-chart.

Encourage people to speak without censoring. You will help this to happen if you stop there being any comments about contributions while the brain-storming is going on, and if you avoid praising, or raising your eyebrows about anything that is said. It is hard to be spontaneous when you suppose everyone has their marking pen poised.

When people have slowed down in calling words out, then give a little time for them to comment on what has been produced. Ask for description rather than evaluation.

Seeing how the words on the chart form groups can help make clear people's instant responses to the idea of leadership. Look for the categories, even using different colours to underline words that people see as going together. Name the different categories, if that seems to help everyone see the slant of their perceptions; even the gaps in their perceptions.

After this phase, which has the object of loosening up energy and letting off steam, ask people to work alone or in pairs, to write down on their own bits of paper the qualities they admire in leaders. If they question you about what sort of leaders, you may find it useful to consult them about how widely they want to apply the word. If you are running a training group for leading small groups, that sort of leader is likely to interest people most. In a group within an industry or other hierarchical organisation, people may want to include managers and other bosses in the idea. When the lists are made, they can be shown in sub-groups or the whole group. Mood, number of people and time available will condition what you choose to do.

At this stage I often discover that people have designed a cross between Leonardo da Vinci, Florence Nightingale and the Buddha. It may be the time to talk about how realistic these requirements are. Are there some that everyone insists on, or others that they might jettison? With luck, some of the more rigid people in the group will begin to question the absolutes in their heads.
One promising direction from here is to look at which of the leadership qualities on the lists are shown by which group members. I like to ask people to recall actual moments when which person has done what, and to give time to hear what the effect was. Once everyone starts looking back in this way, it is likely that they will find that everyone in the group has acted as leader at some time. Then they may want to muse about whether they liked what they did, or how they did it.

This conversation can be described as about the process of the group, or the dynamics. Dynamics simply means forces that cause movement. Different people in the group do this or that, and their behaviour affects what others do, and so on. I like to spell that out, as I sometimes hear people use the phrase Group Dynamics as if it means something quite mysterious, and nothing to do with people.

THE GROUP DYNAMICS

The group dynamics just took over

Group process can be defined as everything that goes on in the group besides the content of its task. The content of building a house is to do with digging, carrying bricks and so on. The process of doing it will vary. A bad-tempered contractor overseeing a mixed group of Union employees and so-called sub-contractors who are workers avoiding tax, will possibly make the process slow and full of bad feeling. A neighbours' co-operative pooling their skills and labour to build their own houses are likely to experience a different emotional and behavioural process, even though they build an identical model to the contractors house. Like most jargon, these words say a useful idea. Like most jargon, they tend to be over-used and wrongly applied.

However, in your small group you may want at some stage to look at all that really happens in the way of leading, to look at the process of leading rather than just assume that it all comes from the named leader.

One very useful effect of having a named leader is, as I have mentioned earlier, to give both the leader and everyone else a chance to discover what standards you all have for leaders, and what unrealistic hopes and expectations are there too. A possibly comforting reflection for you as leader is that if you flail away, and just keep afloat in your attempts at being the godhead, the expert, the fountain of all love and wisdom - then people may not learn much. It is from your and their reactions to you showing your feet of clay that good learning is likely.

This is not an invitation for you to be a sloppy, chummy, avoidant, O-I'm-such-a-goose-you'll-have-to-take-care-of-little-old-me sort of a leader.

What I suggest is that when you feel at a loss, say something you want to retract, develop uncomfortable feelings towards someone in the group, or do whatever is for you Bad Leader Behaviour, that you say so. For me there is a sacrifice of pride in acknowledging that I've made a mistake.

The possible gains include my learning more about what I did, and may not need to do again. Another is learning that the skies do not actually fall; the group does not become Unsafe because the leader slithered on a banana skin and then recovered balance.

Nobody is infallible, even if a leader. One facet of good leadership is, to my mind, acknowledging possible mistakes, and being open to comment and criticism - and praise - of what I am doing. And having the will, in the words of the song, to pick myself up, dust myself down, and start right over again.

4. RULES. DECISION-MAKING. MONEY.

Family therapists have found many ways of looking at what goes on in family groups, that I find very useful in any small group. Some of them believe that in every family, or small group, there are always rules. Even We-don't-have-any-rules-around-here is in itself a rule. So just as you cannot talk without an accent, and you cannot stand without being in an attitude, so you cannot group without having some rules. These family therapists suggest too that in what they call a sick family, the rules are rigid, but unspoken. In what they call a healthy family, the rules are open, and re-negotiated as needed.

In most groups I have been in, we have discovered some or many unspoken rules. Sometimes there is great relief when they are hauled out into the light of day and looked at to see if they are worth keeping.

This rule, like most bad ones, is to do with fear. Mimi has managed to convey that it would be Terrible if she was not allowed all her fads and fancies. Someone needs to be brave to dare call her quite powerful bluff.

Then again, if someone spits on the carpet or swipes another member, it is quite likely that you will all instantly recognise that you had an unspoken rule against such behaviour, and, what is more, that you want that rule openly stated and adhered to. In this case an unspoken rule turns into an open one, rather than withering in the light of publicity.

MAKING THE RULES

When everyone's interest is focussed on rules, suggest that people each write out what they think are the rules operating in your group. In another column they may want to add others that they would like there to be. Displaying the lists and talking them over can give everyone more clarity, and more control of how they run the group. The rules your members invent are likely to be the most creative and appropriate for your group. But in case you want a check-list, here are some areas you may want to consider.

WHO?   Do you want to make a maximum number for the group? Do you want a clear procedure agreed for letting in new people? Who do you want in?

HOW?   Is there any behaviour you want to insist on? Is there anything you decide to forbid? What will you do if people do not observe such rules?

WHEN?   Do you want people to turn up to every meeting unless they're ill or fogbound? Do you want them to turn up on time? To stay right to the end of meetings? To give notice of leaving? It is all very well making up rules around time. The old psychiatrist's joke is that if people are always prompt, they're obsessional; always early, they're anxious; always late, they're hostile; if they vary, they're unstable. Put another way, people's inner time-clocks run differently. You may in your group need to work out whether it will be more hassle to put up with blurred time-boundaries, or more hassle to discipline members to keeping to time. The only good answer is the one that suits all of you, and the task of the group. A rowing eight will be incapacitated by having one person absent. Does your task need you all there at 7 sharp?

In the section on How?, I mention sanctions: what do you do if people do not go by your rules? One answer is, See what we do when we get there. Unless the going gets very rough, that seems a flexible way of living. But a safety net I have often seen to be of use, is to have some clarity about

HOW YOU MAKE DECISIONS.

In your group you make scores of decisions that the whole group goes along with.
It is worth looking at how you tend to do that, and whether you want change. Seduction is one decision-making mode often be successfully practiced.

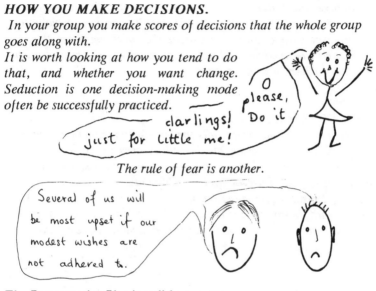

The rule of fear is another.

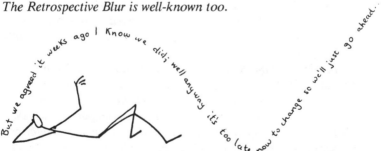

The Retrospective Blur is well-known too.

You can probably add your own titles to this collection.
    Ways of making decisions which are more in everyone's awareness include consensus, through to majority votes and any inventions you may work out for yourselves. Here are two ideas for particular kinds of decision-making, which you might want to copy or adapt.

THE WELSH LEGACY.

In old Welsh inheritance customs, the youngest child shared out all the dead father's goods, into as many shares as there were inheritors. Then the eldest child took the first pick, and so on, till the youngest had the remaining share. Some version of this certainly encourages the making of fair shares. I have used it with students who had to divide their whole intake into little groups to evaluate each person's work. Using this system, they never relegated the carpenters and meanies and wets into one group, but spread them around, to everyone's advantage.

THE DUTCH AUCTION.

In Holland, the auctioneer calls the highest figure he thinks he can get for a lot. If no-one signals, he calls a lower figure, and so on. This system gives no space at all for second thoughts, and can be an exhilarating test of nerves, and possibly judgement.
Taking decisions can be tedious and/or upsetting, in a group of people with clearly different views. I do see sense in knowing at least what decision-making structures are available to use, and too in using your ingenuity to help the process along.

INSTANT READ OUT

John Southgate and some friends once invented an on-your-feet method which has the great merit of giving everyone an opportunity to show themselves.
You start by all standing up. If you are all in the midst of a heated discussion, then keep right on with it. But now, when someone makes a statement of proposition, everyone at once shows their reaction to it. If you are right behind the speaker, put yourself there literally. If you are opposed, stand opposite. If you are vacillating, walk back and forth. If you feel on the side-lines, go there. If you are bored to tears, turn your back on what is going on. At times this procedure cuts out yards of talk, as a speaker does not need to keep on and on, if she sees she has the whole group behind her. People have voted with their feet, in a positive sense.

MONEY

In some groups money may not seem an important matter, if for example you as leader are paid by an institution, or work for nothing. But many group-leaders ask the members for direct payment, and often feel insecure about how to charge, and how to make sure they get paid.

Money is important, to most people for much of their time. How you treat the subject in the group is a political decision. Treating it like the W.C., necessary but largely unmentioned, is well in the tradition of much British education. If you feel embarrassed about money, perhaps that is partly because you did not sit down in school to cost the course you were on, to assess fair wages and other expenses, and to gain some fluency with the symbolic base of the whole economy.

Money is strongly symbolic in more than the most obvious ways. Power, male dominance, love, status and freedom are a small handful of the special meanings people give it. So you are working a rich seam when you allow money to be an open subject in the group. One way to do this is to let the members work out together how to pay for the group. Rent, mailing, refreshments and other costs besides your fee need to be considered. As the paid person, I think the group can require you to say how much you want, rather than having you simper on the sidelines, waiting to have your stipend announced to you. I say this clearly, as I recognise the awkwardness of this taboo topic for many people, and suppose that you are as likely as I am to bolt through any get-outs that are not earthed up beforehand. Another device to stop everyone's evasion, should you decide to work out the members' payments aloud, is to let another member than you take charge of the issue. It is difficult to near-impossible to be dispassionate about what concerns you very closely. So it may be harder for you than for some other member to bring into awareness the evasive generosity, irrational miserliness, or other quirks of your group's attitudes to money-for-the-leader.

Very often, the money decisions of the whole group will be better than your private ones, for two reasons. One is that if everyone makes whatever decision is made then everyone is in control, properly aware of what is going on, and probably in better spirits as a result. The other is that, provided everyone is open about it, you will all know if some members are very short of money. You may as a result find a system of different payments for different members, according to ability and need. I prefer this to my setting a comparatively high fee, which I reduce by so-called bursaries for people who ask. Several heads are better than one for working out this problem. What is more, I am not left alone with the power, uncomfortable to me, of doling out small dollops of bounty to grateful supplicants.

Over the years I have noticed a phenomenon which in my experience has been constant. I do not suggest that it is a universal truth, but it has happened often enough that I mention it here. Anyone who has managed not to pay at all to come to a paying group or course, has been a doubtful asset to the group. Sometimes the group's hard-thought, hard-fought decision to carry a member financially, has been followed by his or her turning up very little, and seeming not to take the group seriously. Sometimes this member who has made herself such a special case financially, wants to be an exception and special in every last way you can imagine, from not taking on responsibilities, to needing many curious favours (the Fluffkin syndrome, see p. 28).

Lastly, a reminder again to you to work at being honest about the money you want, and honest about all your responses around that. What you ask for is to do with how you value yourself. It is also to do with what you need, to pay your mortgage or clothe your children or whatever. It is too to do with what the group members can afford, whatever that turns out to mean, and the current market value of group-leaders where you work.

If you charge a lot, are you being greedy and elitist, or giving recognition to the high skills you have developed and use? If you charge very little, are you putting the work of the other group members beside you into perspective, or are you undercutting? I cannot answer these questions for you. I am not very clear in my answers on my own account. But I see a value in asking.

5. VALUING YOURSELF

Unless I both value myself, and have the sense that some other people value me for at least some of the time, I am not likely to function very well. I shall neither feel very loving to myself or to anyone else. Which is bad news for the people I meet. So having a realistic sense of my value is not egocentric. It is socially useful.

The caretaker at a building where I worked some years ago was a gloomy and revengeful man, who seemed to take grim pleasure in not unlocking rooms we needed, in forgetting to make tea, and generally being obstructive. Several people, enraged at losing lecture time or being unable to offer visitors any refreshment, tried out their self-assertive and confrontative skills on him. The resultant shouting-matches could sometimes be heard right into the next street.

As nothing changed, we changed tack, asked him into some of our course meetings, and began to treat him as the resource he potentially was, rather than as the obstructive villain he had become.

In brief, he then rather quickly seemed to change his image of us and himself. We valued him, and he began to value himself, to the point of feeling generous and involved and actually taking care of us, in the words of his job title.

In another book I have talked at some length about the muddle there is in most people's heads, or somewhere, between themselves and other people. Most of us seem very often to be unclear about who is who. At first glance this is an unlikely idea. You know very well that you will not taste anything if someone else eats your dinner. You know only too well who is going to feel the needle when you go to the doctor's for an injection.

In more subtle ways, though, you are likely as everyone else to have done a few magical swaps. At times you may carry on as if other people will not survive without your attention. And at others you may discount yourself so much that you rely totally on others for approval or validation. Then again, you may negate other people's feelings towards you entirely, antagonise them, and become a bit of a Miller of Dee, like the caretaker described here.

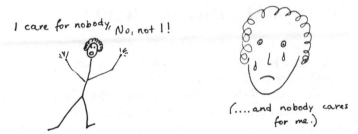

I care for nobody, No, not I!

(....and nobody cares for me.)

It is by and large slightly mad, in a benign society, to discount altogether the value that other people give you. You are part of a cultural group. To be too far divorced from the values of people around you is to be lonely and a foreigner in your own land. To be completely swayed by their values, and their way of valuing you, is to lack shrewdness, and be uncomfortably over dependent.

The happy mean seems to be to trust yourself enough to know and admire yourself, even if you are being misconstrued by other people. What we all need is a realistic sense of ourselves as lovable, in some ways capable, able to give love, in some ways talented and informed and skilful. Then we are likely to feel secure enough to let in other people's perceptions of us. We may not swallow them whole. But we at least have a smell of them, taste them a little, rather than rubbishing them as they are uttered.

Being open about having a good opinion of yourself is specially taboo in Britain. A way to test that assertion is to try the self-validating exercise on page 37.

EXAGGERATE

A perhaps more energising way of doing the same is to take turns running yourselves down:
I'm awful at games; can't run for toffee; never get to a meeting on time; can't answer letters; am a hopeless..;
cont. p.94, as it says in Private Eye.

*Then reverse the exercise, and ask people to make unqualified
boasts, WHICH NEED NOT NECESSARILY BE TRUE.*

*I'm singing Carmen at Covent Garden tonight;I'll
get rave reviews; I won a marathon last week; The
Sunday Times has signed me up....*

*A side effect of the exercise may be to bring to light ways you would
like to be. You may not end up as a Schwartzkopf, but you may
join the local Bach choir and get a lot of pleasure there, for
example. In other words, do not discount even your wild boasts as
nonsense. They come from you, and can tell you something about
yourself.*
*If you have trouble boasting, notice if you had as much trouble
running yourself down. Probably not.*

ROLE NEGOTIATION
*A more serious exercise which aims partly at bringing more reality
into your perceptions of yourself, was invented by Roger Harrison,
and is called Role Negotiation. It will probably take at least a whole
session to do. You need a pen and paper for it.*
*First everyone sits with pen and paper in the large circle, and writes
down everyone's names in a column on the left of the paper. The
rest of the page is divided into 3 columns, headed, MORE, LESS
and THE SAME. For each person, you each write a one-word or
short phrase to describe what you want more of and less of from
them, and what you want maintained.*

NAME	MORE	LESS	KEPT THE SAME
Belinda	Quiet	Smoking	Fooling around
James	Joining in	Despising yourself	Kindness
John	Your clear ideas	Scepticism	Pushing us
Angela	Scepticism	Emotion	Enthusiasm

*In the next phase, you pair with everyone in turn, to tell them what
you have written about them, and hear what they wrote about you,
and talk about all that. You will find that you need to use words
carefully. Belinda may take umbrage at being described as "fooling
around", until she finds that what you refer to is her spontaneity, her
ability to play. At the same time, you note down what everyone
wants from you, so that you get a second sheet of information.*

	ABOUT ME		
	MORE	LESS	KEPT THE SAME
Belinda wants	leading	Sympathy	Listening
James wants	Being noticed	leading	Reliability
John wants	Saying what I'm thinking	Being- for-others.	Laughter

*During these paired conversations, you may want to negotiate with
some people, about monitoring each other. For example, you may
want John to smoke less, and he may want the same. He may want
you to say more in the group, which you also want, though you feel
timid. So you could agree that you will point out when he unawarely
takes out his tobacco; in return, he will actually ask what you are
feeling of thinking, when he is curious to know.*
*The last phase of the exercise is to meet again in the whole group, to
say anything you need to. This is a time to check if people's self-
esteem has been enhanced or temporarily knocked about, and to do
what you need to about that.*

SELF WORTH

*Here is what I consider an important exercise, which is literally
about SELF esteem. Members of the group take turns telling the
rest some of what they like or admire about themselves. Doing this
can bring up great defensiveness, expressed perhaps as silence or
giggles or long rationalizations about the Dangers of Becoming Big-
Headed.*

My response is to state some of what I have written here, about the importance of self-esteem, socially as well as in a more individualistic way. I may add that we certainly live in a culture which suppresses open self-valuing, and that the group-members seem to have taken this cultural message right into themselves. In other ages the heroic boast was accepted to be a necessity if someone wished to encourage himself to heroic deeds.

In other words, I am prepared to push people to try the exercise. When they do it, I encourage the rest of the group, if the speaker allows, to critique what is said, for confidence, honesty, conviction, pleasure, and to persuade the speaker to expand or repeat her words until she feels she had convinced herself, and become one with what she says, rather than in conflict as she speaks.

An extended round of this exercise may be enough to leave group members aware for the rest of their lives of more of their own worth, whether they speak openly of it or not.

6. FEEDBACK

Any few minutes of your or my life probably yields enough material to let us see an enormous amount about our perceptions, our patterns of dealing with people and ideas, our conflicts, and general way of being.

Many of the exercises you do in the group, or ways you behave spontaneously, give you just as much, or more opportunity to find out about yourself, and how you come through to other people. Whether or not you are aware of the fact, too much data is being generated in any group, ever to be dealt with. So what are you going to do about that?

Most group leaders have qualms in their early days, about how best to use these opportunities. You may be so anxious, that you do not make too much sense of what is going on. If this is so, remember that the rest of the group have senses and responses, too. Or, you may be so aware of the layer on layer of possible meaning in any tiny exchange, that you want to rush in five directions at once.

Out of a desire to give of yourself, or from other needs, you may find that you tend to exclude the rest of the group, and give yards and yards of your impressions and judgements of whoever has been in focus. Another early-days solution is to make a "What does the group think?" general invitation to feedback, possibly without consulting the person who will be talked at. Then you keep mum. A prolonged silence often gives an impression of aloof wisdom that has little to do with reality. Notice if you really want to bamboozle the group in this way.

An interesting part of the job of leading, is constantly to improve your judgement about when to be bold and interrupt what is going on, to ask for comment, for feedback. (Notice if you are responding to a sense of ripeness, or more to your own, perhaps frantic, need for whatever is happening to stop. Both motives seem valid, as long as you notice, and possibly confess, which is operating.)

In the longer term, you may want to create an atmosphere in which people feel open to feedback. Remind yourself that very many people have never spent time in public talking about what they do and why they do it, or hearing about their effects on other people.

If you have led or been in a number of groups, you may have grown accustomed to questions like that. If the person you are addressing is new to this sort of talk, she may feel so invaded that she does nothing apparently useful with your enquiry.

By and large, once people are doing something unfamiliar, outside their area of competence, they are more nervy, and even a little dafter, than usual. There is great art in establishing enough sense of safety to allow everyone to function in a somewhat new mode, while steering away from such cosiness that a kind of spiritual sloth sets in. Making open contracts, and setting up guidelines at the beginning of the group, do a lot, to my mind, to help you with this. Another aid is to learn, and then teach the rest, some possibly new ways of giving feedback. Here in this section are some practical suggestions about that.

FEEDBACK

Feedback is a jargon word from the computer industry. It sounds to me like vomiting, so I prefer saying Talk Over, or, Tell Each Other. Some form of these questions may remind people to look at all that went on for them in an exercise or event, and help you as leader to cope with their responses.

1. Check whether the protagonist or protagonists want to hear comment. If Yes, move to 2. If No, to 7.

2. What are your own comments?

3. What did you like about what you did?

4. What did you like about what the other(s) did?

5. What did you not like about what you did?

6. What did you not like about what the other(s) did?

7. (Following no to 1) How have the rest of you left yourselves after that?

8. Do you want to talk? Yes - 9. No - 18.

9. What did you like about what Lucy did?

10. What did you not like about what Lucy did?

11. What did you like about what you did?

12. What did you not like about what you did?

13. What does that say about you?

14. Is there any way you'd like her to act differently?

15. To Lucy, the protagonist: Are there any changes you yourself would like to make?

16. How can you set about that?

17. Is there anything you can do here to begin that change?

18. (Following no to 8) What makes you want to keep quiet? (Indifference? Boredom? Grudge? Fear? Awe? Sense of incompetence to be helpful?)

In no way do I want to set these questions out as a slavish prescription. I put them as a suggestion, as I say, of some of what can be asked, specially in a new group, in a way that gives people room to be competent and useful, and keeps them from too much interpretation, or un-usable comment.

START WITH I

You see, hear, notice, respond to. Then, in ordinary conversation, you are likely to turn those perceptions into what is inaccurately called an objective statement. In a strict sense, objectivity is not possible. You, I always speak subjectively. What you may choose to do is to raise your awareness so that your subjectivity, so that you, are as widely informed as you can be.
A sound rule for giving feedback to people is to tell your perceptions directly, acknowledging that they are your values, your meanings and responses, and are not an out-there definitive statement.
We perceive through a kind of pierced screen.

In speech we acknowledge this in such metaphors as "I wasn't very open to that". "She doesn't get through to me". That screen will always exist. It is each person's way of creating their own meaning. In your group you may let more light through it than before. One way to start that process is to unpick judgements, in the way I have described here.

Another is to let other people's comments in. Again, I see far more use in encouraging people to tell the sorts of perceptions I have suggested here, than in opening the discussion to an interpretative free-for-all.

Remarks like these on the next page are right back to the divorce between the speaker and what is said.

As well as being a very potent route to self-discovery, the way of responding I am proposing here is often extremely difficult for some people to learn or to stay with. I suppose there is at least a momentary high in dishing out gobbets of homespun psychiatry. Noticing words and forms of speech is a constant part of work in groups, and seems a direct way of encouraging precise talk. Here are a few words and ideas I want to beware of, balanced in the right-hand column by those I see as more likely to enlighten.

NO to	YES to
Impersonal constructions:	Active verbs:
It's a pity that	I was irritated when...
It's disgraceful that	I'm angry at...
It's marvellous that	I feel happy
Generalities	
Most people....	Say just who I mean.
Everybody...	Is that I?
One	or
We all	you?
They	or
	My mum?
Always	Last night. Now.
Judgements	Feelings, sensations.
Opinions	Images
Questions	The statement behind each question.
Why?	How?
Yes but...	And

You may want to teach the group to be on the look-out for such habits of speech, so that there is some shared monitoring of what goes on.

If you become very interested in how language affects perception, and indeed distorts it, you may want to read the section on John Weir's Percept language in my Red Book of Gestalt

In this section of this book, let us look further at usual, and then at what may in the group be more useful, ways of responding. If Michael says he feels squashed, he may, particularly if he is young and nice-looking, evoke a rush of protective feelings in some group members. These might show in such statements as:

Don't worry.

We all feel the same.

Lucy didn't mean it, I'm sure

Everyone goes through it.

ACCURACY

One common factor in these is a high likelihood of inaccuracy. How does anyone except Lucy know if she meant it? If he feels bad, then he may need to feel bad. Again how can the speaker know what We All are feeling or thinking at any moment?

Be ruthless in checking your own words, to see if they are accurate. Then see if they say directly, or camouflage what you mean.

It's not important OR?

I don't want you to be upset. AND? OR? I am upset. AND? OR? I like you. Please like me.

When you say Everyone, or We All, or People, you will very often be inaccurate; you will be lying. Say I, and you are more likely to know quickly if what you are saying is true.

Another way of being accurate that I have mentioned before, if making a clear connection between

DATA: YOUR RESPONSE

Time and again in ordinary talk, people leave out one or other. For example, you may work away at encouraging group members to notice the feeling that goes with what they are doing or saying. One odd result of this can be that Feelings take on an almost holy value in the group. It becomes Good Behaviour to Be In Touch With Emotions:

Right on, man.

Really get into that anger.

This is the first real thing that has happened tonight.

In our present culture, where feelings are often suppressed, I certainly see value in enabling people to know themselves emotionally. But, simply stated, a feeling is a connector, a mover. The first e of the word of emotion is an intensive, so the roots of the words can be crudely put as very and move. In other words, emotions get us going. They are the way we move ourselves from a stimulus to a response.

They are connected to causes, to data. Finding the cause of an emotion can be enlightening, and can help whoever is experiencing the feeling to have more sense of reality, and of their own good sense. This is an example of a response, a feeling, needing often to be connected back to the data, the stimulus that made it happen.

Even more obscure are the socially acceptable judgements that most of us utter. In these, both data and response are parcelled up so that you cannot always tell what is wrapped in the gift-paper words. A statement like "You always cheer me up" is a compliment the hearer could learn more from if you spoke more precisely.

Let us assume that you utter it, and then refine it to be more accurate: "You were smiling when you walked in. You looked around at everyone, then straightaway asked me about that interview I was dreading last week".

That is clear data. It is what made you say "You always..." Saying that anyone always does anything, except breathing, maybe, is to be inaccurate. More than that, you may with such a compliment suggest to the hearer what seems to be a very safe activity for her. Encouraged by your blanket praise, she may turn sweeter and sweeter in the group, until she has so deprived herself of any other response that she explodes into being sour. Then everyone may feel confused and let-down.

Spelling out chapter and verse what has made you utter a generality about someone, may make her more vivid to herself. She may reflect that the only person left out of account in her entry was herself. She may be feeling sad, or upset about her own interview, and has channelled that into a camouflage question, by asking about yours.

So another path to accuracy is to look for the statement behind any question. If I ask if you are cold, that is, as you may by now expect me to say, to do with data to my own senses. Perhaps I saw someone shiver. Or perhaps I felt a draught and want the window shut. I am more likely to get what I want speedily if I notice, and say, the statement behind every question I ask in the group. At times, let yourself say the statement instead of the question. It may be more risky.

Here to end this section is a diagram known as Johari's window. It may make you want to reflect on the relative size of the four panes in your own window, and whether you want to alter them.

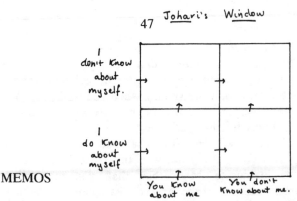

I don't know about myself.

I do know about myself

You know about me

You don't know about me.

MEMOS

Find out if the other person wants your feedback before you present it.

Accept that all feedback given to you is connected to truth, however twistily presented. Or however unwelcome. And note that "connected to truth" is not the same, necessarily, as true.

Telling your own responses, you can speak with absolute authority. You are, or can be, the world expert on them.

Discovering your own responses, you are discovering yourself of this moment, and so are nearer what is real than if you talk generalities.

TISSUES

7. NOTICING AND LISTENING

The last section was mostly about putting out communication. If what you do or say is ignored or wrongly understood, trouble may begin. At the least, one or both of you will be frustrated. Worse, you may become confused. If you go on and on failing to get through, or getting non-connecting messages back, there is a fair chance that finally you will go off your rocker.

We need each other, among so much else, simply to monitor that we make some kind of sense, that what we say is recognisable, and sometimes acceptable too, to the people around us.

Good communication is probably rarer than most of us imagine. I say something that makes sense to me, and instantly conclude that it must make sense to you. You think so too, and suppose you understood me; but you may have missed a word, or have a different sense for a word I use, or think I am referring to a different event than I am, and so on. In the group, there is the chance to check out on what people say, and to allow the possibility of your not being a perfect understander every time.

I was once briefly in a group with Carl Rogers, who in his books has extolled listening as a major therapeutic tool in itself. He says that people are rarely listened to, and that they thrive on knowing that another person at least wants to know what they mean, whether of not the other person understands them completely.

As different people in the group spoke, he unobtrusively shifted how he was sitting, so that he was faced around to them. He did not fidget, nor on the other hand fix them with an unswerving look. He just listened. Soon we let ourselves talk more slowly, and often say less. We were not having to fight for the audience. We

were not needing to persuade or cajole him. We began to listen to
ourselves.

JUST LISTEN

*A child I knew, when told to eat up his dinner, said "How can I put
food in, when my mouth is full of words?" I think it is unlikely that
you can listen to someone else, when you are already full to the
brim with messages of your own. This exercise could be one you use
near the beginning of many sessions, to clear the unspoken words
out of everyone's mouth, and, very likely, to give people the chance
to notice what is really important to them at the moment. Make
pairs, separate the pairs from each other as much as you easily can,
and then take say 3, or 5-minute turns at being speaker and listener.
The task of the listener is first to sit there and notice how you listen.
Rather than impose any oughts on yourself, just notice if you drift
off, or get embarrassed, or focus on some themes more than others,
or are frustrated at not steering the conversation, or anxious that
you are not helping more obviously. Just track yourself, without
making judgements.*

*The task of the talker is to let yourself say whatever you need or
want to say, letting yourself notice and express some of what you
feel about what you are remembering and telling.*

*Notice if you tend to talk for the other, and are wanting approval
signals from her. Or do you cut her right out of your awareness?
One aim of the exercise is to give you the opportunity of being on
your own terms, saying what suits you, and trusting that your
partner will honour the contract of simply listening to you. She is
not going to pull your ideas to bits or tell you you should have
different preoccupations. You may in the first round of this exercise
find out a good deal about your expectations of any listener, and of
yourself as speaker.*

*If, like many people, you are tongue-tied when invited to talk about
anything you like, then you may feel more at ease with a topic.
"What is new, and what is good?" is a cheering up way of scanning
some of your recent life. Or, you can recall your first memories, or
your childhood in general, still noticing the feelings that go with the
words.*

When one person has done that, the other may want to use the same
topic. Or she may like to talk about the listening she has just done,
which is likely to be at the forefront of her mind.
Once everyone has tried the exercise out enough to feel more at
ease, then you are likely to stop needing prescribed subjects.

I recommend this exercise as a general tonic and
prophylactic, at work as well as in the group. One important rule is
that each partner should have equal time as speaker. In that way,
obligations and grudges are less likely, and both people have a
chance to blow off some rage, celebrate some delight, or cathart in
a more muted way, in the brief privacy of the pair.

Listening fully has a good deal to do with openness. But,
rather than try to force yourself into being a kind of human cistern,
into which people can pour out their every thought, you may do
well first to do some selective listening.

SNAPPING SCISSORS

Try out a small experiment to show you something about the
amount of physical response many people have to words themselves.
Ask everyone to think in silence to themselves the words Seven Sets
of Snapping Scissors. Then ask them to stick their tongues well out
and hold them firmly between their teeth, before again thinking the
phrase Seven Sets of Snapping Scissors.
When you have talked about any discoveries people made in that
exercise you may be ready to consider what you listen to, besides
just words. Maybe ask the group to transform what they have been
aware of, besides words, in the listening exercise already done. They
may have brought into greater awareness than usual the double
listening and responding that is universal, but not much talked of.

I listen to your words, tone, pitch, speed of speech,
hesitations, and may notice your facial expression, body attitude,
how much movement you make, and more. As well as doing all or
some of that, I am at the same time listening to, or noticing, my
own responses to your words and to you.

If you and what you are saying seem at one, my body
responses may not be too complicated. If you talk of anger and

laugh, speak of affection and tap your foot, or in far more subtle ways give out more than one message, I am likely to be very busy and somewhat wary, as I try to pick my way through this minefield towards your meaning.

SLOW MOTION
Most of the time, this extended listening is not greatly in awareness. Someone says "I'll just have the feeling you're not happy with what you're saying", but is unable to pinpoint why. What she has certainly done is pick up signals, pick up data from the speaker, which she has translated into what she calls her feeling. Here is an exercise to bring some of that process into slow-motion, for a few minutes of your life, to give you more awareness of what you do.
Once more, work in pairs. Face each other and take turns going through a set of statements. A might begin

> I notice....
> I imagine....
> I feel....

That might make both people laugh, so B might respond

> I notice....
> I imagine....
> I feel......

I put this exercise in the listening section, though you may argue that it is to do with observation, and projection. Which it is, as well. Both of these are part of listening. You may at this point want to talk over whether you believe you can ever disentangle yourself from another person enough to listen "objectively" to them.

PARALINGUISTICS
If you want to, extend the exercise to deal with all the accompaniments of speech I have listed in this section, and which go by the sense of paralinguistics. This time start:

I hear
I imagine
I feel

*An important part of this exercise, as of many, is to spend time
talking through what you have noticed, and seeing if your
imaginings are in line with the other person's reality. She may, in the
invented example, turn out to have a sore throat or a cough, rather
than be suppressing words. On the other hand, she may not even
know that she keeps clearing her throat, let alone know what she
does it for. In this case there is perhaps more adjusting for her than
for you to do.*

LISTENING IN 3'S.

When you are listening to someone, or in a conversation,
you in a sense become part of a system. There are connecting, or
partly connecting, signals and responses going back and forth
between you, in looks, words, attitudes, and probably a sort of
muscular mime right though your body.

Some years ago researchers filmed and recorded very
young babies, while grown-ups were talking. Seen in slow-motion,
the babies' movements looked like a sort of dance to the patterns of
sound, rather than just being the uncontrolled wriggles and
stretches I had seen them as before.

This suggests that we learn to make elaborate body
responses to each other's speech and presence, well before learning
to talk. Most of us have at least some awareness of this continuing.
One way of showing anger and a refusal to join in with someone's
ideas or plans, is to sit quite rigid while they talk. Both people,
perhaps silently, generally register this as punitive.

*Inevitably, you are more familiar with the way you usually influence
any talking than with other ways you have not tried out. As a way
of heightening your awareness, work in 3's for this exercise.
Two of you go on trying out any of the paired-talking exercises
already described. The other one focuses on the pair as a system. At
the end of a 3-minute or so interchange between the pair, all three
take a few minutes to talk over the experience, rather than the
subject of the conversation.*

In the last section there is an account of the sort of questions that might be useful here, or after any of the experiments you try out in the group.

STRESS-FREE LISTENING

To finish this chapter, here is an exercise in letting in sounds, rather than listening. Learning to do this more may help you and the rest of the group to be less tense, fuller listeners.

Relax, perhaps lying down rather than sitting. Let yourselves be aware of the sounds in the room. In your body. In the street. Notice your own body's response to different sounds. Notice where in your body the sound seems to affect you. Experiment with simply letting sounds go through you, without trying to fit images or emotions to them. Imagine a circle round you made by your hearing. See, without trying, how far you can hear. Again, experiment with letting in, rather than straining for, sounds.

Putting on a quiet music tape for part of the time can help make this exercise pleasant.

8. INTIMACY, ANGER, AND FINDING WHERE YOU ARE WITH EACH OTHER.

I define intimacy as letting myself be close to other people, and still being freely myself. Not so easy. What I am describing is different from the gestalt "You do your thing and I do my thing", which at worst is a sort of alienated, individualistic hedonism. Nor is it the saintly living-for-others which means that I am so busy interpreting what I think would be good for you or what I really ought to be doing for you, that I have a very impoverished sense of who I am. (One result of this is that if you are living-for-others in my direction, you will not be likely to make very good guesses at what I want, since I am such an indistinct figure. So we all stand to lose.)

The word intimacy can be a euphemism for love. I do and do not use it in this way, so I had better try to explain myself a little. To justify doing this, I tell myself that as leaders of small groups, you must have assumptions about how people work and what, if anything, we exist for. The clearer you are about these beliefs, the better you are likely to communicate. The more clearly you communicate, the easier for other people to grasp your intentions and know what you are about. The better their sense of how you tick, the more likely they can see more of their own beliefs, and how they themselves tick. So here, more baldly than I might ever state them in a group, are some of my underlying beliefs.

There is a continuity in the universe which I can call a dance of energy, lesser in what seems inert. like rocks, and greater in whatever we call alive, like birds; but there is always rhythm and patterned movement. Between people, all one species with a common evolution, this vast shared likeness is love. What prevents a sort of harmonious ecstasy of recognition of this underlying sameness and love between people is a perverse result of our struggle to survive.

Physical survival is greatly to do with getting enough food, drink, clothing, shelter for this body, for me, not for the generality of the species. So, psychological survival is perceived often on the same model. Erich Fromm in " The Art of Loving" points out that it is much commoner for people to brood about whether they are loved and lovable, than about how easily they feel love towards others. In other words, we tend to be preoccupied about how many strokes, how much approval, esteem, recognition, love we are getting. This insecurity keeps us from giving out very radiant and continuous signals of love towards others. So, feelings of spiritual hunger become widespread. And hungry is angry.

What I am saying is that I believe love is the underlying connection between people. It always exists; but a great deal of psychological hunger stands in the way of recognising this. In no way do I say this moralistically; it is my description of what I see.

A consequence of what I call the psychological muddle is that I have no confidence that everybody all the time, or some people any of the time, will experience themselves as loving. What I hope will result from doing some of the exercises in the following sections, is that group members gain a more vivid sense of self, and more energy. See what happens.

Intimacy is potentially enhancing for everyone. So what else keeps us all from it? Partly, I think, that feelings are so heightened. I shall feel angrier and more hurt and more dejected, as well as more beatific, more joyful and more elated, if I let myself be intimate with you, than if I turn down the volume knob of emotionality, and settle for cautious distance.

More primitively, I guess at a fear of losing myself if I let myself be totally exposed to, and therefore perhaps totally overrun by, your self. In one way this looks an unrealistic fear. The experience of intimacy is of being freely and newly oneself, on one's own terms.

To your intellect the fear may seem unrealistic. But it must have come from somewhere. Rather than condemn yourself for irrationality if you find you shrink from closeness, find what memories or images or fears come to your mind. Like many people, you may find that what other people called love, in your early childhood, was a barter that did indeed involve your being invaded, taken over in some way.

"Mummy won't love you if you're naughty" for example, may be a message that caused you extraordinary conflict. Perhaps it was yelled by a scared young woman who saw you as a bold tyrannical mischief-maker she was getting little support in trying to turn into a socially acceptable child. Your picture, more likely, was of her as some kind of Latter-day All-Giver and All-destroyer. I some senses, parents or their substitutes are the origin of all love for each child. In the strongest sense, the withdrawal of all love is torture of the psyche. So, no wonder if you draw back from an investment in other people which experience has suggested may end up in your having to conform to their ideas of how to behave, if you are to feel love from them. Being yourself is important too.

And yet. The paradox is that I can sense a curious loss of self in being most myself. What I think I lose is my persona, my handy kit of I-am-the-person-who-always-does-X and who-never-feels-Z. I am left with myself not as a description, but as my functioning from moment to moment. The headiness of this experience is often too much to take.

However, one of the likely outcomes or asked-for-outcomes, of working together in a group, will be to overcome some barriers to intimacy, and probably to be intimate more often. If you are old enough, you will perhaps remember those Sunday paper court reports which included the excitingly shocking phrase "Intimacy took place". Here maybe is another clue to why we avoid intimacy. It sounds like sex, which to many people sounds like a bunch of trouble.

Rather than settling for my thoughts on the subject, you may want to ask your group to say what being intimate, or being close to people, means to them.

SCULPT

A less wordy way of doing a similar task is to ask one person to place all the others as near to or as far from herself, as she feels them symbolically to be. Rather than getting into discussions "Well that's not right. Really Jim's close to Audrey", and so on, invite any commenter to make his own 3-dimensional picture of the group in the same way. I see this exercise as a step towards intimacy. It is a saying where you are with people at the moment.

At the moment. This phrase is important. If you in your group are like many people alive today, you may have quite limited experiences of being open with each other. As you experiment in the group you will at moments sense some bed-rock of trust within a pair or larger number. If that is a rare experience for you, then one development may be a surge of good feelings quite out of the ordinary.

On the other hand, someone may seem to be insensitive, or in some other way to violate the delicate first leaves of trust as they grow. He or she may then attract bad feelings which again seem quite out of the ordinary.

All of you in the group will increase your skills and your wisdom, if you find ways to let members acknowledge the sorts of feelings I mention here, and talk them out and through until they are in perspective.

But, as I say often in this book, most of us have not been trained to be good communicators. We often swallow and suppress feelings towards each other, until these are like a tank full of fuel that could better have been used to fire our lives in small sparks from moment to moment. Then a slight jog, one stimulus more, and the tankful blows up, into a vast explosion of good or bad feelings towards what or whoever is standing in our eyelines at that moment.

This experience can be very disruptive for both people. Its opposite, which is common, is at least as damaging: first there is a friendship or more intense attraction between two people. Because A so values B, she decides to overlook his forgetfulness, and does not speak of it. Because B so values A, he decides to be very understanding about her slight bossiness, and does not speak about it. As time goes by, each discovers some other little irritations, too silly, it seems, to mention. The affair or friendship, instead of deepening, starts to shallow, and perhaps finally dries up altogether.

Another end, often, is that finally A or B explodes or collapses over some tiny last straw, and both partners are unable to manage their bad feelings in a way which works through the hurt or rage of the moment to some clear air, and a better-negotiated way of behaving to each other.

Some theorists make a distinction between red and white anger. White anger is perhaps the last defence against panic, and is to do with annihilating, with making the apparent cause of hurt vanish into nothing. It is the walk-out, the sacking, sending to Coventry, refusing-to-deal-with solution.

Poured through the same sieve, or sieve-ilisation, red anger can often appear more frightening than white, because it does show so much. It is to do with re-establishing intimacy, where white anger is to do with trying to get rid of it. Red anger can be the grab, swipe, yell at, I'll-show-him, I'll-give-him-what-for, demanding, solution. The actual or imagined presence, not absence, of the target person, is of lively importance to the speaker.

In one way or another, anger at someone is often a disguised acknowledgement of intimacy, of the amount of power the angry person has glimpsed in the other, the amount of threat and promise that other is to the angry person.

DRAMAS AND SCENES

So what on earth do you do if people get angry with each other in your group? From what you know of them, you may be clear what course to take. If not, here are some general guide-lines. Let them acknowledge what is going on. Let them be angry, rather than try to smooth over their feelings.

Be aware that some people who often get angry, or often provoke anger, are, partly unconsciously, keen members of the Drama Triangle.

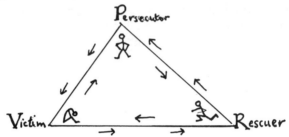

Check whether you are joining in as Rescuer. You may argue that any attempt at clarifying or peace-making is bound to be a rescue, or be seen as one. You can probably work out yourself when you are playing Rescuer in a dysfunctional way, rather than doing a job of work proper to being group-leader. The Rescuer tends to have a high need for harmony, or for being seen as peace-maker, or even in some way to have fairly urgent emotional involvement in controlling the scene which is unfolding.

One of the tiresome aspects of the Drama Triangle is that the players often swap roles and then continue play. So the Rescuer can quickly be seen as Persecutor, and end up Victim. You are more likely to keep this fate at bay if you see the fight as theirs, not yours.

Here is a sketch of some possible needs and responses. It is a portmanteau way of outlining what I have found useful ways of intervening on different occasions.

You: Do you like what's going on? *P&V: No*

You: What do you want to do next? *V: Just stop, forget it.*

You: You're crying and red. And you want to forget it. What about P? *P: I want this out!.*

You: It? *P: This load of fury.*

'You: . Try out unloading some of this fury onto a chair or cushion.

When P has done so, as floridly as she likes, she is more likely to know what she still needs to unload at V; which may not necessarily be much bad feeling at all. Or P may still have large real grudges about V. and V.'s behaviour, which by now will at least not be mixed up with P's general load of fury. Only directing feelings at inanimate objects seems to me to avoid reality. Only directing feelings at people in the room may be just as unrealistic. In a workshop like yours there is the opportunity to do both. Part of your work as leader is to let everyone have a say:

Y: You've witnessed all this, V. What are your needs now? *V: Well I do feel a bit misunderstood.*

Y: What feeling is that? *V: That P. just picked on me.*

Y: What's the feeling in you, towards P? She's on your mind. *V: She just hasn't heard what I meant about the Labour Party.*

TIME TO UNDERSTAND
At this point you may want to push V. more to notice her feeling. Or you may decide it will be more productive to suggest a slowed-down discussion between the two people who are against each other. Each time one of them makes a statement you intervene:

You ↓

OK, A. You've heard B. So tell her what she said. When she agrees that you've understood her, then tell her your response. Then she will tell back what you meant.

MOVING PICTURES

Much of this chapter has been about helping people towards closeness. Distance has value too. If your group is interested in noticing how far or near everyone feels from everyone else, you can make a sociogram, or moving sculpture.

All you do is stand up and move so that you are nearer the people you want to be near, and farther from those you want to be farther from. Everyone does the exercise at once, so you are likely to keep moving! As ever, you need to make some talking time at the end of the movement.

SLS

Another way of showing where you are is to play SLS, or Sibling Lover Stranger. First learn the signs for these, for instance, Sibling can be an upraised arm, Lover a hand to your heart, Stranger the showing of the palm of your hand in front of your face. Then all mill around. As you meet in pairs, simultaneously make the sign appropriate for you. You may have some confirmations or surprises. An effective way to stop people feeling loving towards each other can be to tell them, openly or covertly, that love is their duty. So I recommend that you look out for any climate of obligatory good feelings that starts up in your group, and see that it does not develop into an oppressive Silent Rule.

Be more loving, you pig!

9. BRINGING OUTSIDE ISSUES INTO THE GROUP

Your group may seem disastrously good at carrying out the title of this chapter. Talking about your boss or the dog can be a great way to avoid the unfamiliar, even embarrassing task of being fully present in the group, and recognising and telling what is going on for you in this moment. It is just as arguable that only being present, only dealing with your present feelings for Fred and Daisy here in the group, can be a way of turning your back on the ham-handed or devious ways you deal with people important to you outside the group.

In most interpersonal groups, people gain a lot from an interweaving of what they are doing and feeling at this moment, with talking through some of their past and future life. I think that part of the leader's job is to educate everyone in the group to know better how to do this interweaving.

In the first place you need to censor or comment on yourself when you talk about outside issues, and work out the relevance of what you are saying to the present. Something here made you remember or imagine or generalise or deflect, or whatever you are doing. The others may be as shrewd as you in seeing this process of connection or disconnection.

In many groups in their early days, people are from many causes a bit tongue-tired. If a member volunteers a bit of her history, or a Problem, there is a great temptation for everyone else to swing into the saddle, jam on their homespun wisdom hats, and gallop out on the advice-giving trail. They want to join in, they

want to show their concern, and that is the way likely to be familiar
to them for doing so.

DOING IT YOUR WAY
*The group, at its simplest, gives everyone in it the chance to notice
how they behave there. By and large, there are only two ways people
can behave; they can go on in their ordinary way, or act differently.
So at many moments, questions along these lines can be useful.*

*Do you like what you're doing?
If not, how do you stop yourself doing something different?
How would you like to change?*

*The second question is important, and is not a rhetorical sneer. If,
for example, I keep deferring to people when I don't want to, it may
be that I was so knocked about in childhood for trying any other
mode, that I have got stuck, out of fear. Acknowledging that fear,
and so acknowledging that I function on a remembered inner
rationality, rather than mere weak silliness, is probably necessary
before I can move on.*

NEW WAYS
*Then comes the next step, of imagining doing something different.
For other people in the group, it may be simple enough to suppose I
would be cured, would be myself, or whatever, if I just told so-and-
so to shut up. What on earth makes me sit there tongue-tied?
The answer is, very likely, that I have such a rigid push-button
response of deferring, that I literally cannot imagine myself doing
otherwise. One way of moving forward is to have other people, who
find it easy to stand up for themselves, show how they would
respond in a similar scene.*

Rather than have them just talk, ask them to set up a role-play. Have whoever was bullying or interrupting re-play what they said, and let the volunteer voice her or his responses. When one or two people have played the scene in their way, let everyone discuss what worked and did not work, in terms of effectiveness, and the feelings everyone was left with. Then let the deferrer, who has sparked off all this exploration, take the role taken by the volunteers, and try out their lines and gestures, with as much coaching and adapting as she asks for.

EXCHANGING SOCIAL SKILLS

A formal exercise for everyone, which will help make clear that most of us are pretty blank about one or two social skills, begins with people talking in twos and threes. The whole exercise can fill at least a session. They will need 20 minutes of half an hour, in which to tell each other what it is, which involves other people, that gives them difficulties. One person may dread arriving at parties, another fails to complain to shop-assistants, even if cheated on change or weight. Another may pick fights or quarrels in a way that does nothing good for her or anyone else, or lapses into day-long sulks when snubbed.

The task then, still within the half-hour, is to see which horror for one person is something more easily handled for another. When this has been sorted, they all make sure they have a fair picture of particular episodes of each other's social ineptness.

Back in the whole group, people now take turns in setting up role-plays for each other. For example, Maggie is scared of parties. Jean is not. So Jean briefly introduces Maggie's problem, then, perhaps, asks the whole group to be a noisy party, with Maggie sitting watching. Then Jean comes into the party as Maggie has said she does. The role-play stops, and Maggie has a chance to say something about her feelings, and about how she would like to behave at the party. The group then re-plays the scene, and this time Jean plays the Ideal Maggie, making a different kind of entrance. Again the role-play stops, and if she is ready to, Maggie then takes her turn at being the Ideal Maggie.

This exercise requires empathy, imagination, decisiveness and co-operation, all of which are pretty sure to exist in your group, and may have needed a way of being expressed.

Let me stress again that intelligent, capable, profound, skilled people can be quite blank about how to do or not do something or other that comes easily to many others. This is often difficult to believe of other people. Then when you recall your own need to get out of the bathroom before the toilet stops flushing, or the way you feel bad if you do not phone your mother every three days, even though you have nothing to say to her, then you may feel that you are in those ways particularly weak or stupid and beyond help.

Most of us have some blanks in social skills. Some of them may be related to distress in our pasts, others to a simple learning gap. How do you learn to be at ease asking a policeman the way, if your parents both dived for cover at the sight of navy blue?

Working in the way talked of here, is to tackle a difficulty at the behavioural end. At many other times in the group you are likely to deal with the other, the motivational end.

As I have said elsewhere, we are all applied psychologists. Many people seem too to behave like amateur psychiatrists: diagnosing, explaining, and only talking ABOUT what they see as their own or other people's malfunctioning, often in ways which tend to preserve rather than change what is going on.

I'm sure she's much happier not knowing how we react to her.

There are many ways of changing from this sort of conversation to some experimenting which may be of more use to the speakers. With luck the onlookers will have a more vivid experience too, than if they had no role except to assent to the remarks in the picture.

66

In every case, the overall effect of what I suggest will be to change something

THEN and THERE
to
HERE and NOW

That is the strategy, and you may invent your own tactics to carry it out. Here are some I find valuable at different times. As with every experiment or exercise you ever think of doing, begin by making sure that the people concerned actually want to work, want to understand or change, or do both. Then you might suggest one of these courses:

LIVE STORY.
Tell that episode again, but in the present tense, as if it is happening now.
You will very likely need to remind the speaker at first to keep to the present. If she agrees, invite others in the group to help here with what she is telling, by acting with the story as needed, being the bad mood, tramcar, flock of rooks or whatever is salient, and ALWAYS staying aware that the speaker's experience is the central focus, rather than their own creative additions, helpful as these may be. When the telling is done, see what has changed for the speaker through the telling. Let other people say what looked vivid, or what seemed missing in any way, and see from this what needs to be done next.

WALKING STORY.
Choose yourself someone to listen, and walk around the room, arm-in-arm if you wish, and tell your story, saying what your feelings are about what you are saying, and the people you are talking of.
This can help someone timid to feel befriended, and so deal with their scare of speaking out in the group. Moving about often helps emotions into awareness.

Other people will notice what makes the speaker speed up or falter or stop dead, and can if asked put in this information at some stage. Psychodramatists sometimes begin in this way. The continuation is to set up what seem the most significant scene or scenes from what is told, again letting the rest of the group be appointed to roles by the protagonist, as the first teller of the story is called. Or the group can improvise their way in, as in the Live Story. Check what the protagonist wants out of all this. Talk together in the whole group after the telling, to see what she has made of what has happened, to see if there is more to do at this moment, and to do it. As often, part of your job as leader is to point and underline what is going on. See if the way the story-telling has gone is in itself an example of the sort of scene the speaker told of. Most of us have a great capacity for giving ourselves the same emotional outcomes in widely different settings.

CONCRETE STORY.

Use chairs mugs, oranges, books or whatever else is to hand) to show the different people you are talking about. Place them in relation to an object you choose to be yourself.
Placing things can help clarify a story for the speaker and the listeners. Paying attention to the distances these things/people seem to be from the teller and each other, often brings her needs and feelings more into awareness. She may need to use less words as she feels more of the emotional reality of what she is talking about. Changing the places of some of the objects may be a useful next step. This could be to show how the speaker would like to make changes in her world, or what change she fears. If you suggest this device of using things rather than people, notice what made you do it. Did you respond to a sense that the speaker was confused enough to need a literally objective reality to literally put her in touch with her story? Were you unwittingly joining in with the speaker's distance from the group and reluctance to ask help from them? You need to ask yourself such questions, sometimes aloud in the group, sometimes silently, to stay as effective as you can.

ROLE REVERSING.

Sit over there and tell what you have just told, as if you are X.
X may be the person the speaker was talking about, or else someone
else in her life that you have a reason to think matters in this
context. I sometimes suggest doing this when I have the impression
that the speaker is out of touch with her effect on other people.
Even as she rails against X, you and other group members may be
raising inward eyebrows, imagining how ghastly life may be for X
with this speaker around him. Sometimes, as X, the speaker will
quickly see the other side of the story. Sometimes she will portray
extreme anger or other bad feelings towards herself. The group and
you need to use your best judgement at this point. Is the speaker
realistic, knowing herself to be up against a toxic person, whom she
simply, though perhaps painfully, will have to learn to deal with? Or
is she splitting off all her own bad feelings, and posting them into
the plausible dustbin of a mildly rude or careless relative or
colleague? One way forward is

THE EMPTY CHAIR DIALOGUE

As X, say what you need to, to you. Imagine that you are sitting on
the empty chair opposite you. Talk directly, using I and you. When
you have said what you need to, change chairs, and reply to X as
yourself.
In this imaginary dialogue, the speaker has a chance to see both
points of view. She may go further, and begin to see how far the X
she portrays is a real other person, and how much this internalised
X is an aspect of herself. If this is the track, then she probably
wants to continue the conversation, moving between the chairs. See
that she does, and that she does not revert to a third-person
narration from one place. If the speaker can sense a clear
separation between the characters in each chair, she may well need
to see them as more than just Awful in one chair and Pure As The
Driven Snow in the other. Get her as herself to say what she needs
from X, and as X, what she needs from herself. See what the two
are prepared in imagination to give each other.

You may in this way help the speaker to bring life and flexibility back to too rigid and mutually hostile aspects of herself, and to integrate them in a new way.

If she cannot sense much difference, or show much difference, between herself and X, that is the work point. She is being vague about where she stops and other people begin. Until she can sense that separation, she cannot work towards any new integration. She is pushing clouds of fog. Enabling her to recognise what she is doing is probably quite enough for one session, without going on to the dialogue I have described.

As ever, your job is to enable, not to disable. Very occasionally you may come across someone who is extremely unwilling to do this sort of exploration. You may be well advised to respect their unwillingness. If you yourself had a very cloudy, a very hazy sense of who you were, you might be scared to start blowing on the mist, for fear of it all disappearing.

As leader you are doing well if you make a creative suggestion, have it turned down flat, and stay aware of the refusal as part of the speaker's whole meaning, rather than just its effect on you. Your first impulse may have been to feel a fool for not saying the right thing, or to get your gander up and determine that you will not be beaten. Scrapping probably would turn out to be being beaten, in the sense of losing overall awareness. So how do you win?

Winning is being fully present and whole-hearted. So, if you are a self-revealing leader, you may want to say the effect on you of being turned down - without using that comment as a way of making the speaker feel bad, or feel constrained to do as you suggested. If your way of working is to say less about yourself, you may just point out what has gone on, how the speaker has made a block in proceedings, ask her if she often does that, or ask other people how they feel in response. There is more on this in the chapter called The Stymie.

Similarly, there is much more about this empty chair work, in the Red Book of Gestalt I wrote. Here I am sketching out a number of ways of bringing what may seem to be about life outside the group, right into the present.

ALWAYS AT IT

An effective way of doing this, without any special structure or exercise, is to ask the speaker and, if he agrees, the rest, to see if they notice likenesses between what he is talking about, and what he is doing at the moment. If, for example, he is complaining of never being understood at home, see if he is being understood here. Perhaps to him the word understood means noticed, or cared for, or allowed to have the floor, or get his own way over things. See what he thinks is going on here. Perhaps people are getting restive at his complaining, and do want to fob him off or make him be quiet. How does he trigger that response? Does he do the same at home? The tool in such an exploration is everyone's careful honesty. In the same example, if the speaker feels that he is well understood in the group, then check that that is indeed broadly so. Then ask him to work out what he does here that makes for success, that he does not do at home. Again, other people's memory and insight will probably help his own. He may attribute his success here to the good character of everyone else in the room. Does this mean that everyone at his house is horrible? Well, this is possible. What has he done to make or keep them horrible, that he does not do here? It is his role in all that goes on that can help him to see how he influences the responses he gets from people. Encourage him to look at himself, instead of talking again about others.

MEMO

Check what makes someone talk about something outside the group.

What makes it present for them now?

Maybe they just want to tell it.

If they often do that, negotiate how long everyone agrees to let them talk.

If they want help, ask them to ask for it and stay in charge.

Very often, any device which makes the out-there event seem as if it is happening in the present, helps the speaker experience more vividly.

10. THE STYMIE

If you have led groups, you may recognise the sense of having been handed a blocking answer or silence, or a comment which kills all action dead. What you were probably responding to, if you did get such a feeling, was the speaker's wish to do just that: to put the brakes on something she found extremely uncomfortable.

Your working life will be more fascinating when you come to the discovery that stymies are potentially very fruitful to work with. It was a revelation to me long ago when I learned "you can't not-communicate". If I sit rigid and withdrawn, or turn my back, or walk out, these are all communications. In rather the same way, there is never nothing-to-work-with in a group whose task is partly to look at what is going on for its members. If someone drops a symbolic portcullis on proceedings with her, that portcullis is likely to rattle down on to someone else's foot: other people are bound to be affected by her in their idiosyncratic ways. Giving them time to talk that over is one valid next thing to do.

You and the rest of the group need at such a moment to be very aware of yourselves, to know whether moving on to deal with someone else is simply a way of escaping from the discomfort of dealing with the first speaker.

An important bit of work here for you as leader is to be sure that you or someone speaks of any such new twist in the story of the group. Revealing the Process is a jargon phrase for this.

POETRY

Just now we seem to me like a herd of sheep baa-ing along behind a new ram. What picture do you have of what we are doing?

Images are often the most vivid way of expressing part of what is happening. Ask for them. Give time for them to be heard, and for more to form in the poetic part of people's minds. They may be more vivid and enlightening than intellectualising, than I-think-it-was-because talk.

To explore more of the wealth that an apparent stymie creates, let us make an example by pretending Lucy has just had a sharp quarrel with Emily, snubbed Michael and, among much else, said that the group is very uncaring. She follows this by saying no, she does not want any comment from the group. If you are a beginner at leading, you may at this point wonder what on earth to do. She may have roused angry feelings in you, as she almost certainly has in a number of others. Indeed, people may start voicing their bad feelings, in spite of Lucy's veto on comment. You may let them, from whatever motive. If you do, you may find yourself noticing that the group is sounding as uncaring as Lucy said it was. This is worth pointing out. The follow-up could be to ask people to recall what else they have done which Lucy might have seen as uncaring. If she used the word, she must have had grounds for doing so.

By going along the path of looking for what is valid in Lucy's accusations, you may stop an escalation of defence. At best you will begin a process of disarming, which will give everyone a chance to acknowledge more reality. You will need to judge how far you think it useful to screen Lucy from more unsolicited responses from the group. From what she said, she sounds very insecure in the group. So a bit of firm boundary setting by you may give her some confidence. She may not necessarily be ready to admit this straightaway.

On the other hand, if she has repeatedly behaved like this, you may want to consider how long you are all prepared to go on being treated so hurtfully. You have an ultimate sanction, which is not likely to be easy or popular, of refusing to have her in the group. (If it is an easy or popular solution, then Lucy was probably spot-on in her accusation of uncaringness, and you as leader may want to rub everyone's nose in that fact.) I mention this sanction, partly because it is likely to dart through some people's minds, but not be voiced. There is often an unspoken rule about throwing people out. Like all unspoken rules, it is often best brought out into the light, to see how it looks and feels when openly spoken of.

Long before getting to such a surgical remedy, you may do well to try and bring to the surface much more of what is going on.

Is Lucy the only person present who easily shows anger and other bad feelings? If she is, then you all need to pause to consider what a convenient little creature she is. She expresses all the nastiness in the group, so no-one else needs to be nasty. If there is anyone to bawl out or screech at, Lucy will be sure to do it. And if the rest of you want to express bad feelings, you can always turn them into a tidal wave of righteous wrath at Lucy. The way you indulge all your own bad feelings is to suppress and condemn her bad feelings. Hm.

Or, is Lucy somehow producing in the rest of you some of the despair of sense or helplessness, the rage or frustration that she often feels? Perhaps speak of this idea, and use it to let other people get a sense of what it is to be Lucy in her bad moments. If this insight is accurate, it is likely to lead other people to feeling gentler with Lucy, and perhaps finding ways of communicating some good feelings, which seem sparse for her, in her direction.

The chapter on Valuing Yourself deals more extensively with some of what I have been saying here.

Now let's have a detailed look at alternative ways of being direct with each other. In everyday life, being straight with Lucy might be seen to be uttering such about-you but not-about-me messages as these on the next page:

There may or not be some truth in these remarks. Whichever is the case, they are unlikely to give Lucy much interesting, welcome or usable learning. What all three statements have in common is that they are exclusively about Lucy, and leave out any direct mention of the speaker. All this is fine if what everyone wants is a fight.

SAYING WHAT YOU MEAN

If, as is likely in the group, people are concerned to learn more about themselves, a good place to start is to see what is making them want to pronounced these resounding condemnations. What are they feeling in response to what she has done? Ask them to be precise as they answer that question. Be on guard if they say:

"I feel that she ought to...."
"I feel that nobody else here...."
"I feel that I'd like...."

None of these are statements of feeling, of emotion. They use the word feel more as if it means think. The major clue is the word that following the verb. Feelings can be stated much more simply.

I feel angry
I feel frightened
I feel happy

These are direct statements of feeling, which are what is asked for here. So there is a clear message in the syntax of the sentence itself.

The word THAT after I FEEL will not produce a direct statement of feeling. If it is possible to insert THAT after I FEEL, and still make sense, the sentence is not a direct statement of feeling.

Feeling accompanies and probably generates all your behaviour and your speech. Find out what you feel and your perspective on what you have said may change considerably.

Group members may even have convinced themselves that the judgement they passed in telling Lucy what she ought to do, was the product of pure clarity of vision, mixed with a little general altruistic feeling for The Group. Finding out that they are really very angry with her, may suggest to them that they were over the top in speaking on behalf of everyone, for example. The speaker was certainly affected. Others may not be.

MAKING CONNECTIONS

If you find that someone is very angry, or very any feeling, then a possible next question is What else, in the rest of your life, is making you feel like that?
Have you expressed your feelings, or done something useful for you with them, in those other places?
I have made up an example of anger, rather than delight, because many people find anger an embarrassing or shameful feeling to admit to. The questions are as valid if they are about tremendous, or slight, or absent feelings, of any kind. A sudden huge whack of feeling can be a clue to someone's not having an opportunity either to feel, or to act usefully on that emotion, in their life outside the group. Insight about this will at best lead to some changes in what he or she does.

A possible side benefit of this sort of investigation in the group, is to give Lucy the chance to go through the same process inside herself, then or later, whether or not she is prepared to talk about it.

So there is another response to the block or stymie. I think it takes effort not to be totally put down by someone who is doing their level best to put you down. After a good deal of experience, I find that as leader I choose generally to say I feel humiliated or inadequate, if I do. But I do not see much use in stopping functioning just because of that. If I did throw in the towel, I might well be punishing Lucy and getting others to gang up against her. I would be making a covert statement like "Now look what you've done! You've upset the LEADER! You've ruined the session!" I would as well be making myself incompetent, and so giving my self-esteem a knock.

Besides these considerations, it is also true that I am often, not always, a bit less upset by sabotage attempts nowadays, than when I started working with groups. The sabotage, as I am calling it, now tends to alert me, even excite me. It is a challenge: a clue to some perhaps difficult, but potentially rewarding work for us all. Provided I do not lose my marbles.

GIVING YOUR CONTEXT

In a practical way, here are some possible moves for you to make, if you do feel very upset, and want to use, rather than wallow in, the feeling.
Assume that Lucy or whoever can hear you, however out of touch she seems. Do your best to fill out what you are saying, with more aspects of what is going on for you. You will but rarely tell the whole truth of what goes on for you, because so much complex response is there. But in this sort of group you have the chance to notice and say what lies under and alongside your first statement.

"I was frightened when you spoke so loudly and said what you did." (This description of what went on is painstakingly factual, and can be checked easily with other people's perceptions. If you use a more colourful "turned on so-and-so", "barked at", or "lashed out", you are implying heavily that Lucy's motives were aggressive, without giving any space for her to contest that except by denial.)

"I suppose I imagined that you might do the same to me. Perhaps I was frightened that I'd just wither and collapse if you did. I know that would not happen. But that was the fear."

"I was scared that I'd be so angry with you that we'd fight to death. And I don't want either of us to be annihilated."

"I'm bad at doing anything useful with my anger, so I was frightened I'd just silently hate you from then on. I'm glad I'm not being silent about it, even though I feel embarrassed."

"I admire your passion, and spontaneity. I'd like to learn them from you, but don't know how."

"In my head I know that if we have no conflict, we'll have a pretty insipid group. In my feelings I panic and want to smooth over any sign of bad feelings. There've been too many of them in my life. I need some help from the rest of you to sort all this out."

There are many more responses that you, all of you, may find, if you let yourself notice you, your real emotional response, the images and memories that are evoked by those feelings, and the way of coping you were choosing or evading.

Near the beginning of this chapter I suggested that there is always something going on in people, however much they deny or do not notice it. In less florid moments than the incident with Lucy, you may feel just as much at a loss when someone says they feel nothing and need nothing. I sometimes come across groups of fledgling psychotherapists or counsellors who in private twitter like sparrows over such people, uttering condemning cries of Blocked, Defended, Heavily Defensive, Damaged, Fragile, Hostile. These words are meant to be descriptions of the Nothing-er in their group; the words could roost nearer home, too.

In general I do not see much value in grandiose diagnostic words, when they are used to comfort the speaker, rather than make a bridge to the person being talked of. At worst, talk like this begins to create a fantasy world of jibbering loonies, where only the professional owns and expresses sanity. What tripe.

So what are you going to do about this person in your group who sits on her hands, silent except for the odd cutting remark, or the odd weak little admission that she does not mind, no, it does not matter to her at all what everyone wants to do, she will just sit there?

THE SILENT MEMBER

Here are some possible things to say. They are not meant as off-the-peg statements for you to learn by rote, uncritically. They are sketch-plans of different approaches, to bring into awareness different facets of what may be going on.

"You haven't spoken for a long time, and I'm worrying myself about that and about you. The longer I'm quiet, the harder I find it to say anything, and I wonder if that's going on for you."

"How are the rest of you affected by Colin's silence?"

"I could paraphrase some of what people said, to something like 'You have a duty to communicate in this group. You are supposed to have good feelings towards the other members. You are not working, you are only a passenger, if you are not talking.' Is that what you heard? Do you agree? What's your response?"

This could lead to Colin's defining some of his own expectations, and maybe his disgust with himself at not fulfilling them. Doing this, he would be contributing, and probably gaining confidence. Or it could lead the others to see if they will put up with a member who does not behave like them, and so perhaps to notice their covert intolerance of anyone's not conforming. It may, at extremes, lead to Colin's leaving, or the group throwing him out.

*He may just be in the wrong place in your group, in his own
judgement. Or he may be such an infernal nuisance, so antagonistic
to other people's hopes and assumptions, that they decide to push
him out. Assuming that that does not happen, here are more ways
of dealing with his not joining in.*

*"Colin, I sense that you are not at all used to this sort of group. But
I see you always turn up, and you seem to take in a lot. You smile
or look sad in response to what other people say. You look as if you
are working. Would you like just not to be badgered, not to have the
limelight on you for the moment? Other people have said they like
to hear from you. So do I. But do you want to settle for being an
observer for a couple of weeks, and then we check what is
happening? How do other people feel about that?"*

or to a different Colin, or a Colin-at-a-different-time:

*"You say you have no responses, nothing to tell. If you put a bio-
feedback machine on yourself, you would see what a remarkable
amount of response you have to a change in voice tone, a look, to
everything going on. So I believe you do have feelings and other
responses. At the same time I can believe that they are outside your
awareness. Do you want them to stay out of awareness. You've
heard the effect of that on other people. But do you want to stay
that way? There must be some advantage for you, or you would not
have settled for being like that, I suppose."*

*Having stumbled at last on what many other people had been aware
of for thousands of years, which is that people are so cussed that
they will often do the opposite of what you suggest, some
psychologists have given this bluff-calling the highfalutin title
Paradoxical Intervention. Except in spontaneous moments of rage
with my friends ("Good! Yes! Do go and drown yourself, and good
riddance!") I do not go in for deliberately manipulating people's
natural-born pigheadedness.*

*I mention all that here, however, since I often notice, and often with
surprise, that when someone hears their awkward behaviour
accepted or validated, they no longer cling to it, but throw it out. So
the effect, if not the motive, may be paradoxical intervention.*

Carl Rogers maintains that nobody changes until they have
accepted themselves. So long as they are carping and criticising
their behaviour, that behaviour seems to dig in its heels and fight to
stay around. When they can look with some understanding and love
at what they do, perhaps seeing the old hurt or hope that made
them first act that way, then they can often change what they do,
even without much conscious effort. For intensely nervous group-
members, some acceptance and empathy from others may at times
melt their inner carping and allow the same thing to happen. Group
disapproval might just be an intensification of their bad feelings
about themselves, and an inadvertent strengthener of the rearguard
fight of their sharp tongue or whatever. Your task may be to make
clear that you are acceptant. If you are.

MEMO

Your feelings at the stymie are a likely clue to what is
happening between you and the stymier and the others: You may
be mirroring her feelings. perhaps you need to check.

Or

You may be caught as other-character in an emotional bind
the stymier often generates. Let your and her and other people's
judgement help you check this possibility.

Or

You may be feeling what the stymier has anaesthetised
herself not to feel. Anyone who is silent or bolshie has good cause
to behave so uncomfortably. And yet that does not mean that you
always have to put her needs before yours and other people's.

11. CONFRONTING

I was angry with my friend:
I told my wrath, my wrath did end.
I was angry with my foe:
I told it not, my wrath did grow.
W. Blake

This section is about confronting people, and, importantly, finding what to do then. One outcome of confrontation can be to release energy and good feelings towards the other, and yourself. But it takes two to tango. If the other person will not respond openly, you are not likely to get closer. However, you will have said where you stand and what you want. You will be clearer about your own position. You will also have told your wrath, and stopped it growing into Blake's Poison Tree. And you will have made yourself clearer to the other person. He or she can learn from that.

In your group, members may be very interested in the topic of confrontation, and each recall people, possibly outside the group, they would dearly love to confront. Pause at this, and notice if you think of confrontation as always negative. In its origin, the word is to do with being front-to-front, face-to-face. This can mean head-on; it can also mean tete-a-tete. For our purposes, let us broaden confrontation to mean saying your direct response to someone else, about how they seem or about what they do, no matter whether that response is rewarding, punitive, warm, angry or what all else.

CHOOSING WHO TO CONFRONT

As a first experiment, ask people to find a partner to work with. At the same time, remind them that the topic is confrontation, so ask them to notice how they choose. Give them a few minutes in their pairs to talk over how they got together, how they felt as they do, and how they feel now. Ask them to tell each other whether they confronted each other, or whether they colluded. I use the word collude to mean "going along with" in a way that avoids discomfort rather than being an honest expression of what you need or want. They may want to return to the general group after this, to recount some of what went on in the choosing, and possibly, to choose again.

SILENT REHEARSAL

A next exercise is for the pairs to start by facing each other, standing. Explain that the exercise is silent, and is a chance to notice some of their feelings and sensations to do with confrontation, without going any further.
Other questions will probably come to you as you look at their expressions and body-tensions.
When you feel ready, ask them to recall, still with their eyes shut, how far they seem to be from their partners, and then to shift if they need to, to the distance that is comfortable. Only then ask them to open their eyes, to check what has happened. Now, still in silence, let them move again if need be, to establish a "right" distance from each other.
Now as they face each other, ask them to notice something they like or admire about the other person. When they have done so, they again shut their eyes, and imagine themselves telling this bit of praise to the other person. Ask them to notice how they imagine feeling, what their voice sounds like in imagination, and where they tense muscles. Let them think about whether they like the way they imagine delivering the message, and then if they wish, let them change their tone or words or attitude in silently telling it again.

At this point, give them ten minutes or more to sit down together, with the task of recalling and telling what went on, specially in their emotions, during the exercise. Ask them specifically not to tell the content of the imagined confronting statement. There is a good deal else to deal with: how familiar the feelings were; how they sensed their bodies at different moments; how easy it is for them to be at ease, face to face; whether they were more preoccupied with what the other person might be thinking, or with their own role; how they would like that balance to be.

CONFRONTATIONAL IMAGES
If people are enthusiastic, they can move now to another useful bit of co-operation. First, partner A finds how she wants to stand to confront B. And she places B the way she wants him to stand while she is confronting him. When both partners have tried out this arrangement, they tell each other how these physical attitudes affect their feelings to each other. Then B initiates, finding how he wants to stand to confront A, and how he would like A to stand while he is doing so. Some comparisons between the pairs may be illuminating.

YES! YES! NO! NO!

CONFRONTING WARM-UP
This exercise could be used to make a different warm-up to the session on confrontation. Have the group form into 2 lines, facing each other. In their lines, they hold each other, arms round backs. The 2 lines face each other. Line A keeps saying of shouting YES at line B, who keep responding NO. This exercise may become and stay exhilarating and laughing. (Watch for anyone getting more rattled, and if they do, give some time for them to say what memories or fears have been evoked, and to find what they need to do about that now.) Line B should also have a chance to shout YES, to NO from line A.

*As ever, people need a chance to talk about their responses to this
apparently simple task. How did they feel about shouting, and being
shouted at? Did they want to win? Do they feel they did win? What
does winning mean for them in this context? (John Weir once
defined winning as doing whatever you are doing with the whole of
yourself.) How did their feelings change from the start of the
exercise to the end? Do they value NO differently from YES? Did
they feel better saying one word then the other?*
There is a lot to think over.

In most groups I think you will need to do some of the
above exercises, or similar, before going on to the next stage of re-
learning confrontation. I say re-learning. Many people have over-
learned either a flight response: they just do not confront anyone
ever; or they may have accustomed themselves to emote, blame,
complain, squawk or moan, in a way which does not change what is
happening. What can be noticed in this next exercise is more of
each person's personal style of confronting - still without talking.

ANOTHER DRY RUN
*Once more, ask people to pair and face each other. When they are
standing as they want to, reassure then that they will stay silent,
then ask them to look at each other, and find at least one point on
which they want to confront the other. Suggest that there is always a
potential confrontation between any two people. Both have
responses they can say or keep quiet about. As these people know
each other to some extent, there is likely to be history between them
which is not resolved, appreciation or resentment which has not been
uttered.*
*After a minute or so, ask them to shut their eyes, and imagine
making their confrontative statement to the other. Ask them to
recall the tone of voice they imagined using, and to notice their
feelings. Did they sound convincing to themselves? What did they
imagine would happen if they had spoken aloud? What did they
want to happen? Ask them to change or re-run the message if they
wish.*

Now let them open their eyes again, and in silence part from that pair and find another person to confront. Go through the sequence again, asking them to note differences in their feelings or sense of effectiveness with this new person.

If the group is small, you may choose to let people pair all round the group, discovering these points of confrontation. At the third pairing, suggest they deal with more aspects of confronting. It is possible that, so far, the confronting statements have been expressed only as judgements about the other.

JUDGEMENT UNPACKED

As is explained elsewhere in this book, judgements often become more accurate, and possibly more acceptable to the accused, when they are unpacked and expanded to show the speaker's part in what is going on. Not everyone finds it easy to do this translating of what is probably an emotional statement anyway. So here are two detailed examples.

Judgement: You're marvellously thoughtful.
Now what behaviour, preferably very recent for the sake of clarity, makes the speaker give this summing-up of the hearer's character?
Data: You gave Anne a book, and you had my photocopying done for me.
Since the speaker noticed and remembered these actions, they seem to have some emotional charge for her. What is it? Let us imagine.
Speaker's feelings: Grateful. And anxious.

Now we come to the important reality of what the speaker wants from the hearer. I will go so far as to say that if there is no demand, then there is indifference generally. Intimacy is to a great extent to do with wanting from the other, and negotiating each demand.

What might be the wants in this invented example?

*Demand: I want to go on trusting that you will bother about me.
And. I now notice I want you to be generous to yourself as well as
to the rest of us, or I may feel forced to do endless little jobs for
you, the way you do for me.*

More briefly, here is one person's expansion of the

*Judgement: You're really arrogant.
Data: You stared out of the window while I was talking to you.
Speaker's feelings: Angry. Powerless.
Demand: Look at me while I'm talking! Reassure me that I at least
make sense, and that I have some interest or value for you.*

*In the exercise, you may do well to ask people to find their
judgement of the other, and then, with their eyes shut, take them
through the three unpacking statements in turn.
When you judge right, ask people back to the main circle to tell
what they want to about their own behaviour in the exercise.
Encourage people to say more about what they judge an effective
confrontation to be like, and to notice in what parts of that they
have self-confidence, and in what parts they feel less secure.*

My view is that a confrontation is not very satisfactory if
you stay at the barking dog stage, of making a loud or fierce noise,
but do no more than that. I hope to work for a shift of perception
in both people, an in many cases, a shift of behaviour too.

One of the many ways this ideal is prevented, is because
uproar occurs. If you say you dislike what I do, then I may feel so
furious, recalling my frequent forbearance (cowardice?) over your
conduct, that I rush into verbal revenge. So you dig up another
grievance, and I counter with four more. Then one of us rushes out
of the room or throws real or verbal frying-pans. Reconciliation, if
it comes, will probably be to do with soothing the vast distress we
have caused each other again. What a relief. However, nothing has

been done to deal with the cause of the original confrontation. Trouble will come up again.

FIGHT RULES

So what is needed? See what the group decides, in terms of making some workshop ground-rules to help teach yourselves confrontative skills. Some groups I have worked with have usefully decided on a clarification stage. This may be best explained by an illustration. We can continue with the "You're really arrogant", example. The initiator preferably does not at first state this judgement, but confines herself to the concrete you-did-X, I-responded-Z, as illustrated. She then gives her hearer, whom I will call Ned, a right of reply. Ideally she does not do this by fixing him with a hawk-like eye and demanding "What have you got to say for yourself?" The conversation may be more rewarding if she, whom I will call Millie, can express a bit of cautious humility. Let us run through a possible development of this confrontation. Millie states her feelings, response and demand, then asks:
Millie: What was going on for you?
Ned: I felt embarrassed. You seemed so intense, I think I was trying to keep from getting sucked in, or something.
Millie: Do I seem that intense now?
Ned: No. I'd say you look a bit upset. And I feel O.K. to look at you.
Millie: I think I got intense because you looked away. I was trying and trying to get through to you.

In this instance the speakers are now getting through to each other. They showed enough self-control to go on looking through what has gone on, and report honestly in a way the other can hear. It turns out that the first judgement was based, as often, on a misunderstanding, which they have cleared up.

FIGHT MANAGER

Now let us play the scene as if Ned is a good deal more defensive. You as leader get a role in the conversation.

*These illustrations are far briefer than is likely in reality. But I
hope they illustrate a few tactics and useful interventions.*
Millie: *What was going on for you?*
Ned: *I don't think I was looking out of the window.*
L: *Let's not get into a yes-you-did-no-I-didn't. Ned's not aware of
doing what Millie says. Did anyone else see what was going on?
The group agrees that he was staring out of the window for part of
the time she was talking.*
Ned: *Well I think better looking at the sky.*
Millie: *First you say you weren't staring out, then you say you need
to stare out!*
*You notice that Ned's defensiveness is rattling Millie, not
surprisingly. Do you want him to get a public lambasting? If you
do, then sit back for a bit. If, on the other hand, you judge that his
rigidity would soften, to his advantage, with a bit more support, or if
you want him to have a chance to assert his own ground, you may
perhaps speak again.*
L: *Millie, you've told Ned what you want from him - a bit of
interest, some valuing. And it looked as if it took quite a lot of
courage to say it. But I'm not clear about whether Ned actually
wants to go on with this. You don't have to, Ned. What do you
choose?*
Ned: *I want to stop.*
L: *It's worse for you to sort out what Millie's upset about, than to
live with knowing she feels like that?*
Ned: *Yes.*
L: *OK. But she is upset, and I want us to give her a chance to talk
that through anyway, even if you don't join in much.*
*You have respected his decision, but not let him shut Millie up. And
in the ensuing conversation, part of your job may be to see that the
group does not shut Ned up if he wants to join in. But let us go on
with the example, assuming that Ned says, a few lines back:*
Ned: *I'm prepared to go on. Except that I get the feeling that the
whole group's ganging up on me.*
*This may be near the mark. By pointing out what is going on,
though, Ned may have changed it. If you like, you can invite the
group's co-operation with him in a practical way at this point.*

L: So far we've got stuck on the staring out of the window. Millie's expressed some feelings, but Ned has not said his, directly. What about letting the rest of the group help as they see fit? If anyone suspects they can usefully extend what Ned or Millie are communicating, then double them. That means going and standing behind one or other, putting your hands on his or her shoulders, and speaking as if you are that person you are touching. When you have spoken, go and sit down again. How do Ned and Millie feel about that?

They agree. There is silence. Someone goes and stands behind Ned. This device is warmer and more lively than just being observers. It is often called doubling.

L: Put your hands on his shoulders. (She does so]
D-N (Double-through-Ned): I feel self-conscious and stuck. I've never felt at home in this group and now I feel I'm being punished.
M: (Starting to cry) I'm the one who feels punished. He just seems contemptuous of me.
L: Talk to Ned, not about him.
M: You seem contemptuous of me.
N: Well that's your problem. (Consternation in group. Silence.)
M: I just feel awful, and confused. I wish I'd never started this. Hm. Confused? Does that mean hostile? Are her tears mostly to do with getting the group on her side. One group member seems to think so.
D-M: I want a lot of valuing and interest in this group, and I'm very good at getting it. People spend so much time appreciating me that there's less attention left for you, Ned. Is that how it seems to you?
N: I just wish she'd get off my back.
L: You, not she. (Silence.)
D-N: You scare me stiff, Millie. In fact, I feel awkward with all the women in this group except Pat. I'm lonely.

M: *It's very hard for me to cope with that bit about getting all the appreciation. I think there's something in it, and I feel so ashamed.*
L: *What are you saying to Ned?*
M: *I don't know. (With shame.) That I'm so greedy that everyone's got to be nice to me every minute or I'm just in pieces. Stupid. I really want to stop now.*
L: *What about you, Ned?*
N: *It was never my show.*
Group member: *O Ned, that's exactly the way you always get everyone's back up!*
L: *Hang on. Not everyone: you. And I don't want to go on. I can see feet wagging, and I doubt the usefulness of a round of Uproar at this moment. Ned, did any of the things people said through you, as doubles, seem to be accurate?*
N: *Spot on.*
L: *You don't talk much, do you? Half the time I'm trying to shut people up to give the rest a chance. With you, I always want to hear some more. Do you want to hear more from the group now, about how you come through?*
N: *I don't think I could take it.*
L: *One of my hopes is that everyone in this group gets better at taking care of themselves. One test of that is whether you give yourself headaches or sleepless nights after the group. Just now I stopped people talking. But it looks as if there's a lot of feeling around. What do we want to do about that, in the twenty minutes left?*
In this illustration I've shown a confrontation which did not end in immediate approach between the two parties. Perhaps Ned will never feel much at ease with Millie; but life goes on. The task then for the group is to see how they live with such an outcome. Do people want to force Ned to see Millie's point of view? Or do they want to ignore him, if he will not play by the group rules or norms? Do factions form, one lot understanding Ned, some others joking about him behind his back?
Do you feel tempted to become the super-ego or critical parent of the group, and tell them to be nice to him?

You will do better to say what you think is going on, and ask people if that is what they want. If they do want something different, then help them find how to go about it.
Another way you can be useful, if no-one else steps in, is to ask Millie what she has got out of the episode, and what the others have learned.

SPELLING IT OUT

It is possible that you have some more fluent and volatile members than Ned, in your group. They may quickly engage in arguments which seem intellectual and sterile, merely reinforcing the prejudices of each speaker, and leaving them and others dissatisfied. If they agree, they can with the help of the rest of the group as interrupters and discipliners, try this simple-to-understand-but-harder-to-stick-to experiment. Here are the rules.
A makes a point.
B paraphrases what A said, until A is satisfied that B is really conveying what A means. Only then is B allowed to launch his counter-argument. A now has to tell B's argument until B is satisfied that A is conveying B's full meaning.
And so on.
To do this experiment, each needs to listen properly to the other, and to make some empathic effort. For nervous, intellectual people, this can be hard. You may all need to be patient.

NOTICING THE SCARES AND RULES

The exercise in this section can take a long time, and you may spend several sessions working at confronting, first in a more experimental way, and then going through to points of conflict between group members. A way to strengthen the learning that goes on might be this. When the trumpet and the shouts have died, and the group has moved through a number of confrontations, into a more reflective and peaceful time, ask them to tell their own rules or advice about confronting. Ask someone to write them, preferably on large pieces of paper that can stay around.

As in brain-storming, write all the rules, whether people agree with them or not. Then let everyone note down their own private set of procedures, incorporating as few or many of other people's ideas as they like. If these are shown around, more can be exchanged and learned at this stage, too.

Confronting is not a social skill that comes easily to many people. I have seen some value from encouraging people to use their heads as well as the rest of them, to learn more of it. The more analytic members will probably help at this stage, while the more empathic people will possibly have contributed a good deal in the practice of confronting. All are needed.

12. SUPPORT GROUPS.

This title always sounds odd to me. It sounds like Support Hose or Firm Control Girdles. I prefer to use the phrase Like Groups. That is to say, if people decide to meet because they have a common problem or disease or disability or I.Q. or colour or passion for the ballet, what is Like between them is, at least at first, in the forefront of their minds. A certain basis of trust is already there, in the obvious overlap between members.

Some ward-groups, some groups of relatives-of-prisoners, some groups of relatives-of-mentally-ill-people, and others you may have in mind, will probably do well to spend most of their time in sharing experience, feelings, and then help. As leader, you may have learned all about irrational hostility, or Unconscious Group Process or the psychopathology of small groups. Is that what the group wants to learn about? Is it in the implicit or explicit contract of the group? If not, then you will probably keep quiet about some of what you see going on, and will concentrate on enabling the members to build some trust, and to make the group meetings an oasis of encouraging experience in what may be long treks of hard times in the rest of their lives.

I want to labour the point before going on to suggest some activities for Like Groups. People in group therapy form Like Groups. So in a sense do depressive people, or violent offenders. These are a few examples of people who are like, but who are likely to contract into a group where they will be challenged and confronted or interpreted or set goals, as well as listened to. In the Like Groups I am thinking of in this section, the members may not want to examine their own neuroses or learned behaviour in this way. And you, as I say, may need to guard against swinging into action and giving then a no-holds-barred fearless confrontative experience that you can achieve, and which you know has been enlightening and stimulating to other small groups you have worked with.'

So what are these people likely to want? One way to find out is to ask them, at the first meeting, and both listen and note what they say. If the likeness in the group is a phobia, or some new physical difficulty such as amputations of heart disease, then people will often be clear about what they need. They are likely to want to talk over what is going on for them physically, socially, emotionally, and work at adjusting or coping.

But if the likeness is, say being close relatives of long-term mentally ill people, members may be more reticent. They may if the group goes well, later speak of very complicated feelings at the early meetings, of distress, anxiety, suspiciousness, embarrassment at the strange milieu, and guilt. With all that going on, no wonder they hang back.

Structures are a shelter against anxiety, so if you are leading a Like group where people seem inarticulate and have a poor opinion of themselves, I see value in being prepared to suggest things to do, as well as in modelling, showing, some of the good feelings not very available in the rest of the group. By this I do not mean that you become a stage caricature of a brightly patronising Welfare Person.

As I have already mentioned in passing, listening fully is something you can yourself do, and, maybe later, teach. But at the early meetings you may be more use as a clarifier than a teacher. Just as much as anywhere else, your group members will carry with them the needs

to be recognised
to feel competent at something
to get on with people

A first ritual of recognition is some kind of introducing-yourself exercise, perhaps one of those described in Chapter 2 in this book. Feelings of competence may be let in early if members begin some practical problem-solving. Exchanging addresses, explaining the local public transport, or arranging to bring a cake to next week's meeting may be tangible ways that members go about showing that they can be capable and of good will.

I remember a group in which the fathers and mothers of two adolescent schizophrenic girls confessed their despair at how to cope with their daughters on weekend leave from hospital. After consulting the girls and staff, they swapped children for the visits. This solution left the parents with the gratification of showing that they could care effectively for a teenager; they were not the complete monsters they half-feared themselves to be, from reading about madness as a family product channelled through the weakest member.

When a Like Group works well, it often has much in common with a Rogerian counselling group. I have explained a little about Rogers' methods, listening and reflecting, in Chapter 7. His belief is that people function best where they perceive in their interlocutors what he calls

unconditional positive regard
empathy
authenticity

These terms, like Maslow's, need explanation, if you do not speak fluent American. The ideas embedded in them have so much relevance to Like Groups, as well as to being with other people in many contexts, that I will attempt an explanation here.

UNCONDITIONAL POSITIVE REGARD

is a valuing of, interest in, good feeling for yourself or another person, in a way that allows the object, you or the other, to value and accept herself. Rogers makes clear that people cannot force themselves to feel unconditional positive regard. At the times your spirit expands to let you feel it, though, and you can also communicate the feeling, then you are offering what everyone probably yearns for, recognises, and grows by. There is a qualitative change in what goes on within and between people. Fear disappears, and the speaker no longer needs to edit what she says, in case she bumps against the listener's conditions, and stops being approved of.

EMPATHY

is an ally of unconditional positive regard. It is the ability to accept and understand the world in the way the speaker does. This is not the same as identifying, or partially becoming the other.

Identifying is an activity that sometimes gets the slow handclap or the raspberry in psychological circles. I give at least two cheers for it. The once or twice I remember having friends correctly pick up, express and even dramatise my feelings in this way, I have felt flattered and comforted.

In the longer term, though, I see empathy likely to give similar comfort, plus more spiritual space for the speaker to discover her own responses, feelings, needs and solutions to what she is talking about. To demonstrate the concept of empathy, I sometimes ask someone to stand behind another person, with a hand on her shoulder, as in the exercise called doubling. Standing there, you are in contact with the speaker, you are literally seeing from her point of view, and you are likely to sense some warmth towards her. And you are still clearly yourself. You still have to check carefully on whether your intuitions are the right guesses.

AUTHENTICITY

in this sense, means being all of a piece in what you say or
do. If I say O do stay, and simultaneously get up and hold the door
open, you are likely to pick up a clearly inauthentic message. I said
one thing and conveyed the opposite - don't stay another second.

A good actor can lament a dead child or praise someone's
beauty, and be very convincing, even moving. His art is to be
congruent, to have voice tone, gesture, attitude, all making an image
of truth, of authenticity. But he is not being authentic. He may hate
kids, or think the actress he is eulogising looks like the back of a
bus. I mention the professional actor here, as many people have
some of the same skill, and can at times make convincing shows of
feeling which they themselves know are not authentic.

Authenticity is there when the spirit is in line with the
body and the words. It seems that most of us are far shrewder
observers than we are even aware. We mostly know, not only when
we, but also when other people are being authentic. Our whole
response then modifies, relaxes into trust that we do not have to be
on guard.

An apparent paradox follows. It really looks as if people
will function better on, say, open bad temper from someone, than
on that person's pretended patient understanding. The word
pretended is the important one. Falseness makes a bad experience
for the person being false, and the person addressed. It muddies the
path between them. Authenticity may not bring about instant
paradise on earth. But it is bound to clarify what is going on,
certainly for the speaker, and with luck for both. Being authentic,
speaking your own truth, is the opposite of maddening. Sadly, I see
that there is no current word for en-saneing, for encouraging
creative discovery in this way.

The temptation in Like Groups, and not only there, is to
bask in likeness and good feelings, and then when not-likeness and
bad feelings coyly peep around the door, to shift them out and
pretend they do not exist. It is as if a group myth has silently been
invented - that if people in the group have good feelings towards
each other, then they do not have bad feelings as well, at all or
ever. Another way of saying this same myth is that if people have

bad feelings towards each other, they cannot have good feelings as well, at all or ever.

How do you begin to guess if this or a similar myth is taking over? There may be sudden silences, that to you do not seem like a peaceful digestive pause between one happening and another. Or you may begin to suspect that one or two group rescuers keep leaping in with anecdotes or other items, which somehow do not engage people's attention. Smiles may look fixed. Feet may tap.

You yourself are the surest indicator. If you are uncomfortable, and feel that there are things you had better not say, you may be feeling frightened - frightened of one person in the group. or of how everyone might respond to you - of being out of line, unacceptable, not nice.

...and she just gave me this look, so I thought well bother you I thought and I just turned my back....

SNORE

Maurice, I've stopped listening.

Saying something like this may not be easy. Asking if other people feel the same may show that you are alone in this response. Or it may relieve the feelings of other people who are getting impatient with him, too. If you like Maurice, you will probably manage to say a negative to him without upsetting you both. If he gets on your nerves anyway, he is quite likely to pick up your hostility, and produce some of his own towards you.

Be clear, as clear as you can, about what you are doing. You are taking care of yourself. A happy outcome could be that Maurice stops his repetitive complaining, you feel better, and he gets some insight into how boring he can be. BUT your purpose in a Like Group, as I have said, may not primarily be to give the members insight and the chance to change. So what are your goals?

According to who is in the Like Group, I respond from different awareness. Searching for what I generally do in them, I think I work consciously, as I have said, to notice and value everyone's experience. I want people to feel their competence, and to recognise the group sessions as safe. Along with that, I want to be myself, and have some gratification too. So I need to do what I can to keep myself enthusiastic. That for me means that I want to be openly and honestly myself. Believing that the leader, willy-nilly, tends to have a good deal of influence, I also think it likely that if I let myself be false or evasive, I may be encouraging other group members to pretend in the same way.

I remember the man in the cartoon who is looking at the cinema advertisement. "Rape? Bestiality? Violence?" he reads, "No. I can have all that at home." Being phony may be equally familiar to many members, and thus, no kind of inducement to stay in the group or learn from it.

As well as feeling safe and valuing themselves, I also want people to have the chance of saying and feeling some of the hopes, fears, worries, shames, which they may keep quiet about in ordinary social conversations. From doing that, I hope they will blow off some steam, feel more relaxed, and begin to look freshly at their difficulties, and maybe find new ways of coping.

THE DEPENDABLE STRUCTURE

One way into this sort of talk is to have a formal structure. In a group of lonely and very talkative people, you may all decide to have one round at the beginning of the group, in which everyone says a few sentences about themselves, and then to have set times, 20 minutes or half an hour, when just one person is being attended to by all the group. Listening, empathising, and not giving any advice, may suit your group as a style at such times.

If people are tongue-tied, they may be helped by a clear instruction for the round of contribution at the beginning. Some co-counselling teachers use "Tell something new, and something good." I have seen this device cheer people up noticeably, and leave them more robust for dealing with other feelings. See if your group enjoy it. And watch for whether they need a balancing instruction at times, like, "I'm secretly worrying that...."

*By and large, people seem more practised at secretly, (or openly)
worrying over difficulties, than at enjoying their own successes, or
remembering moments of pleasure. So the first instruction may need
to be used more often than the second.*

NAUGHTY TALK

*In a group which seems to be weighed down by very like problems, a
brain-storm can be a good pressure-releaser. Suggest that, without
any censoring, people call out what they would like to do. A group
of general practitioners doing this exercise immediately came up
with, among many others, these statements*

Murder all my patients
Have an hour to each patient
Burn the surgery down
Go to New Guinea
Never sign another form
Go Private, with a price-list on the door

*Here were some very responsible people letting themselves say the
unthinkable. The doctor who fancied murder later tried to discount
what he had said. We encouraged him to notice what pressures
made him feel murderous even in fantasy, and he said that he was
very tired. He liked the New Guinea suggestion someone else had
made, and indeed later went for three weeks to Indonesia.
Many group members lack the funds for this sort of solution. The
point I am making is that every brain-storming statement is worthy
of respect, perhaps as a poetic rather than a literal statement of the
speaker's need at that moment.*

PHYSICAL STRESS REDUCTION

*Another formal exercise which may be of use here is to teach
relaxation. The last exercise was cathartic. After it, and other
shared talk, a session may end with some quiet. There are many
ways to teach relaxation. Here is one, in the form of the sort of
instruction you might give.*

*"Make yourself comfortable. Loosen ties or belts or any tight clothes
if you want to. Shut your eyes. Now tense your feet and calf
muscles, as hard as you can. Hold that. More. Let go. Hear your
breath as you do.*
*Now tense your thighs, and pull your bottom and tummy tight, as
hard as you can. More. Let go.*
*Pull your chest and shoulders in, round your back, hunch up, clench
your fists and elbows. More. More. Let go.*
*Now screw your face up, and tense your scalp and throat, clench
your mouth. More. Let go.*
*Let your breath out in a big sigh, and notice that your lungs decide
when to breathe in. Let the breath right down to your belly; let your
back go wide as you breathe. Feel the breath warm as you breathe
out, and let the breath go a little longer than usual, without forcing.
Just be aware of your breathing, and the darkness behind your shut
eyes. If you need to shift to be more comfortable just let yourself."*

*Simply learning some of their own breathing, and finding ways to let
it be more peaceful, can make vast improvements in their physical
and emotional health. Fifteen minutes is by no means too long for
this, if they are interested.*

FREE DREAMING
*Once people seem relaxed, you may want to give them some guided
fantasy suggestions, partly to keep them from darting back to their
ordinary stream of consciousness with which they usually keep
themselves tense. Here is one such fantasy. You can invent a
thousand yourself. I put in bold type sentences which in my view
should always in included in guided fantasies.*
**"I am going to make a few suggestions. If you want to, go
along with them. If you don't, then tune my voice out.**
*Still with your eyes shut, and letting yourself breathe deeply, begin
to be aware of the group as a circle. Imagine a glow of light round
each person. Gradually watch that light join into a complete circle."*
*(Leave time between each sentence, and at least half-do the exercise
yourself, to find how long you take to form each picture.)*

*"Now notice how far the light from the circle spreads out. Just
follow it, no need to push. Then when you are ready, imagine you
are breathing in this light with each breath. Feel it cold in the top of
your nose, and warm in your throat. Imagine it going down into
your chest. With each breath let it spread further in your body. Into
your shoulders. Down your spine. Up into your head. Into your
belly. Down your legs and feet and out through your toes. Down
your arms and hands and out through your fingers. No need to do
anything except feel the light and its warmth.*
**Finally, when you are ready, bring yourself back to being your
familiar self now, and open your eyes. If anyone wants to, we
can talk about some of what you experienced."**

This can be a peaceful way to end a session. Check if
anyone had difficulty in making the images. People need to be quite
open to do such a fantasy. Respect people's refusal to join in, or
their blankings. Maybe note to yourself that you need to do more
next time to encourage their trust. Paradoxically, that may mean
that you need to respect their mistrust.

LEARNING TO TAKE CHARGE
*Another simple way to round off the end of a Like Group session is
to ask one or two questions about the meeting itself. I do this
sometimes when I am with people who seem unused to noticing or
retaining good experience, or at taking charge. The questions might
be along the lines:*

What's been the feel of today's meeting?
What do you take with you as you go?
Is there anything you want to change next time?
How can we plan to do that?

13. JOINING

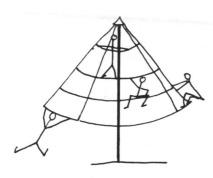

In some recreation grounds there is a revolving frame for children to whirl around on. Before they can 'get it moving, they have to shift about so that the frame hangs in balance. Each time someone changes position, or each time a new person climbs on, others have to shift to make the balance again.

So with people in groups.

The new member's problems may include these: she does not know the history, rules, habits or norms of the group, so she is in this sense incompetent for a while. She is likely to believe that the group is united, and skilled, and also rather hostile to her. She herself may feel daft, unskilled, unrecognised, a bit hostile, and generally windy, as well as having some hope and curiosity and other good feelings.

In a way the group probably is at least slightly hostile to her, as well as welcoming. She may be an asset; but she may slow everything down just by being there, all new. And she may be a threat, somehow upsetting the group balance. In a way you must well recognise, the group is likely to close ranks to some extent, and to appear as united, and as skilled, as the new member fears.

So what on earth do you do about all that? Many times, it seems enough that you make sure the discomforts of this addition to the group are talked of. In my experience, admitting to good feelings tends to strengthen those feelings; admitting to bad feelings tends to melt bad feelings away. So, if you see overt rudeness to the new member, comment, and ask the people concerned for their comment. See' what other feelings are around, too. If you hear nothing but warm welcome, state your surprise at their being no negatives about the large event of having a new member. And, possibly, keep on prodding.

Often, when a group is safe, and the members feel that they are secure and fairly free in it, they will not be very bothered about having an extra person. But if there are low feelings in the group, and a sense of insecurity, this can take members in one of two ways. They may fall upon the new member with garlands and kisses, somehow hoping that he or she will be their saviour. Or they may turn all the hump they have not been expressing to each other on to this as-yet-not-one-of-us.

These responses are to do with the recent history of the group. As well, many people have a strong general tendency to be either includers or excluders. The excluders may rationalise their preference to keep people out, by stating that You Must Have Limits, or that The Group Will be Diluted, or some such. The includers may rationalise their love of new stimulus by saying We Need New Blood (!) or The Group Was Stagnating, or some such.

So who is right? I think they all are. A closed group finally becomes like a locked house, a kind of do-it-yourself prison. And a group which welcomes in all and sundry will begin to have the transient feel of a Displaced Persons Camp. It will cease to be a group, and become a crowd. Theorists have different ideas about how many people are the maximum for a Small Group. Sixteen is often seen as the dividing point. Put simply, a Small Group is one in which all the members can make eye contact with each other without much trouble, and know enough about each other from moment to moment to be realistically intimate, rather than functioning on guesses for much of the time.

If your group has short infrequent meetings, you may begin to lose your Small Group sense at a much lower number than sixteen. I say all this here, to support nature's Excluders, though I admit to being an Includer myself.

Most of this section so far has been about the difficulties for the group in having someone new. The joiner herself may feel so scared or defensive that she has little attention for anyone else's problems. She has an extraordinary amount of work to do, to find her place, to see how to behave, to decide if she really wants to belong, and to get herself recognised and validated. She is, in the eyes of some psychologists, bound at the same time to be going through some of the infantile feelings to do with being the new child in the family. No wonder if she does not feel in command.

Again, you may do enough if you see that she has a chance to make her pitch at the first meeting she comes to, and talks a little about herself and her interests. But some people are so tongue-tied or fazed at such a time, that they do not take the opportunity you offer them. An exercise in pairs, which is new to everyone, may make a safer way in for such a person. For example:

SNAPSHOTS
Start by standing and forming a close circle, with your arms round each other's backs. Spend a few seconds looking at the faces round the group. Then shut your eyes, and notice if you are tense. Let yourselves relax, breathe more deeply, and distribute your weight comfortably on your feet. Then open your eyes, as if you are cameras, taking a 2-second exposure of a face opposite, before shutting your eyes again and remembering for a few seconds what you saw. Repeat this 2 or 3 times to different people, checking when your eyes are shut that you are letting yourselves relax. Then look around the group again, slowly, letting yourselves notice which people in some small or larger way remind you of other people who have been important to you in your life, even in your childhood. Let go of each other and mill around silently till you pair with someone who has stirred your memory. Then sit down with him or her and tell who you are reminded of, and tell too how that other person was or is important to you. See if your partner has a memory which connects to you, or needs to pair again, in which case you move on. Afterwards people can recount anything they want to about this exercise, in the whole group.

People who have attended the group for a while, as well as some new members, may fail to have a sense of being joined, of belonging. As ever, having a chance to say so, is in some cases enough to change their perceptions, and allow then to feel like proper members. Others seem to get more out of a physical dramatisation of how the group seems.

LIVING IMAGE

Ask the person who feels out of things to arrange all the other members the way they appear to her to form themselves into a group. Then ask her where she senses herself to be in relation to the rest, and ask her to stand there. At this stage you may want everyone to say how far they can recognise the image of the group, as having at least some reality in it for them as well as the arranger. Or, you may ask the arranger how she would like the group to be, and to place everyone, including herself, in the new pattern. Make sure, before doing this, that you leave enough time for her to notice all the feelings that go with the first arrangement, the one that is her present image. It is quite likely that she sees the group as a closed circle, or some other tight excluding pattern, with her hovering or somewhat turned away, on the outside. See if she is aware of advantages, as well as disadvantages, in perceiving herself in that relationship to the rest. She may even be reminded of other places and times where she felt the same.

BREAKING IN

If she decides that she really does want to get into the group, then suggest that she finds a way to do so, without words. By this time there are probably strong inclusive, even rescuing feelings, going through many group members, and their impulse will be to give a space. Remind them to think over whether doing so seems more useful than giving the arranger the chance to assert, even aggress her own way in. It is possible that with no struggle, she will have no sense of triumph or achievement, either. But that is not a rule. It really is a matter for each person's best judgement. If the break-in does not feel right the first time, you can always do it again in different ways, perhaps with the help of other members' ideas.

108

14. SKIVING. LEAVING. ENDING.

If people in your group pay much attention to their feelings, they may well be surprised at the amount of emotion they have over anyone's being late, or not turning up. In their heads they can rationalise about bad public transport, or a cold epidemic. In rest of them they may notice moments of irrational rage or punitive urges.

Silent

Thoughts

People probably feel that they have worked very hard for the group, have given time to the missing person, and now are rejected by him or her. So the members present have been labelled valueless. What is more, they also have to find how to go on living in a group which does not seem safe any more.

It is easy to feel a magic in the presence of everyone. Everyone is The Group, who had the spectacular bust-up last week, or showed such insight and compassion about something very painful for this person or that. Now if one person is away, what will happen next? Perhaps four will absent themselves next week.

It is in the interests of the group's survival, I think, that members get steamed up on this issue and begin to discipline each other to attend. Added to all this, if they have felt annoyed with the missing person when she was present, they may now be feeling horribly guilty. Fritz Perls suggests that guilt is just resentment turned back on yourself. This may be a moment to see if that feels true for any group members.

A next move, after feelings have been vented, could be to work out some rules or recommendations about turning up. The Rule section may help you do that, insofar as it can be done. Turning up to this sort of group is probably far more to do with each person's priorities, than with any rule. Because everyone recognises this, the insult of not coming along is keenly felt.

The feelings people have around absentees are connected with the pattern of complicated emotions around death, or any parting of significance. The most significant parting in the group is likely to be its ending, so I will say some more about what are usually labelled mourning or bereavement feelings, in case you want to see how they are dealt with in your group, as it nears its end.

Before that, see how important you let endings be. One way of avoiding them is to have a group which ploughs on for years, through generations of members, who never leave all at once, which would make the group's death a plain fact. There are benefits in this style of Immortal Group, which outweigh the value of dealing overtly with ending.

You may run an opposite sort of group, which bowls along merrily until Sudden Death, the day you decide to emigrate, at which point you ring all the members up and tell the group no longer exists.

Another possibility is to have an open agreement with the group that it stops at the end of term, or Christmas, or some other defined date. Even then, it is possible that if people are very absorbed in other matters, ending will not be a major preoccupation. In other words I do not think that the leader has a duty to rub everyone's nose in How They Deal With Ending, as some therapists insist. But members can, if they want to, learn a great deal about themselves in this phase of the group's life, so you will be properly equipped if you are aware of some of what is happening.

GROUP PROFILE ON ENDING.

As soon as people know how long the group is going to last, they deal with that knowledge, probably by methods they copied or invented a long while back in their lives. Some time in the last quarter of the group's life, ask people to signal if they know when it is stopping; not to say when it ends, but whether they know. You could then ask all who think they know to stand in one part of the room. Then check if the Knows were right, and write up on the score sheet how many were mistaken. You may even want to distinguish how many thought it ended earlier, and how many thought it ended later than the correct time.

Then ask people to write one word to describe their present attitude to the group's approaching finish, and to mill around displaying their words, and clustering with people carrying words with similar meanings. Again, write up the scores under headings that everyone understands.

According to the size of the group, you may want all to talk together at this stage, or to work in smaller clusters. The subject is The Group's Attitude to Ending. That is to say, you are looking at the group as if it is one organism. The different votes are like different perceptions within one person. Working like this can help people accept that it is possible to have several different strong feelings about ending.

SURELY EVERYONE FEELS THIS WAY?

After this exercise, members may want to go on and look more at their personal feelings, at what makes them "forget" when the group is ending, or what makes then cross off the days impatiently. If they feel only gloomy at the impending loss, what keeps then from happier feelings? And vice versa. Is this how they have dealt with leaving parents, spouses, jobs, parties? If certain people experience only the dark or bright side, or seem immovably indifferent, they may want to role play. Ask them to exchange attitudes, so a sad person tells how good it will be to be without the group, an indifferent one tells how painful it will be, and so on.

So how do the theorists, who have studied dying and bereaved people, and see the little death in any parting or change, think people tend to react? In short, they see stages in dealing with loss. One is anger, partly to do with loss of control. Your life stops being the shape it was if your lover walks out - or if you marry, come to that. The change is frightening. Fright there is no effective way of dealing with easily flashes into anger, which is sometimes an expression of impotence. Anger near the end of a group can be from a thousand causes; but one of them could be, at some level, at you for setting the death date, or at the world, including the all group members, for upsetting a pattern of life.

Another stage of bereavement is denial, which also shows as bargaining. in the group this may come out as, "We'll all meet at Sheila's birthday next week anyway", or "I think it would be a very good thing to have some Review Sessions spaced over the next few months." You may hear many creative versions of the central statement here, which I take to be something like, "Please don't let the group die just yet."

Nor is there any urgent need for a group to stop just because you expected it to. It is your job to help people see whether they want to continue because there is plenty of life in the old group yet. Or whether they are going to odd lengths to avoid ending, so as to avoid too the possibly vivid pain and pleasure of bringing the group to a close.

In a group where the members have set themselves to find out more about how they tick, they are likely to gain insights about their habits of responding, right up to - and beyond - the ending of the group. As leader you may be the person to keep them focussing on what they are about, whether they seem to see the group as a sinking ship from which they try to scamper, rationalising as they go, or on the other hand are trying to persuade you all to become a residential community.

Much of what I write here about ending the group, appli to people who leave during its life. From time to time someone moves house or gets ill, or has some other change in their life which, for the leaver and the group, seems to warrant their going. Then there may be honest regrets on both sides, and not too much emotional disruption. More uncomfortable, perhaps, is the departure of someone who in some ways has not seemed whole-heartedly present. Blame and guilt may start to buzz like wasps around their going. I see it as your job to help people notice all that is going on, and too to do anything that they need to.

Sitting in the group making interpretations about the skiver or leaver's reasons, may have short-term benefits like cheering everyone up, a bit the way people cheer up in pubs and buses if they tell each other what they would like to do to the Prime Minister or some mass-murderer who is in the news. But the person no longer in your group may have difficulties in which you and others in the group are more involved. You need to work out whether you want to leave her to stew in her own possible discomfort, or whether you want to deal with some of yours by getting in touch. However cross or despondent someone is, I assume that she can hear, she can still read. So even if I don't get a charming answer, I can communicate. My self-esteem may then rise and I shall feel less frustrated. She may feel better too.

It can be a hard and productive piece of work in the group, to decide whether you have done enough vis-a-vis the missing person, or whether there is use for any of you in going on communicating.

ACTION AS CONFLICT RESOLUTION

Here is an exercise for pairs, which might be useful at a time when someone has threatened to leave for emotional reasons. On the face of it, it is mostly intellectual. As well, it can be a path to striking insights, and a good deal of empathy within each pair. You need about an hour, or even more, and paper and pen.

Person A works as scribe for B and also directs the beginning of the exercise. The first task is to help B relax, perhaps as I have suggested on page 100. Then A asks B to scan idly back over her life, looking for important actions she has taken. "I got depressed in my teens" does not count as an action in this exercise. Actions are specific.

Caning father when he tried to cane you, going to college, taking a
job, leaving home, giving up spinach, may be important actions in
your or B's life, in your perceptions.
As B recalls, A jots down these actions on paper. When B has found
enough, maybe eight or more, the two work together. Now the task is
to look at each of these actions as if it is the solution to a conflict,
and to puzzle out the two sides of that conflict. Everyone's conflicts
are different. You may well notice several, which are suggested by
just one action or solution.

I needed to be a good girl

SOLUTION
I got married at 17.

I liked sex

I was scared to leave home

I wanted to leave home

When the pair have worked though several actions, finding the
conflicting motives that seem to lie behind them, they go to the next
stage of the exercise.
This is to look at how the solutions match the conflicts. Often, only
one side of a conflict is dealt with by a solution. Often, too, clear
Habits emerge, of which side of that sort of conflict is suppressed,
and which side is dealt with. There may be occasional Contrary
Solutions (as in Mary Mary Quite Contrary). Someone who keeps
doing things just to please his mother is likely on occasion to do
things just to spite her. Neither the Habit nor the Contrary Solution
does too much for his own real satisfaction. This happens in
Breakthrough Solutions. These are actions which deal effectively
with both sides of the conflict.

SOLUTION
I became a music-critic

I love opera and concerts.

I can't sing or play a note

*Seeing the conflict beneath a proposed solution of leaving the group
may, in this exercise, help someone see whether leaving would be
Contrary, a Habit or a Breakthrough for them.
When B has finished, she becomes scribe and aide generally to A,
and the pair work again.*

Very often, the ending of the sort of group we are talking
about in this book is poignant and painful for most members. They
may have revealed more of themselves, been more of themselves,
felt more cherished, felt more for others, than is at all usual for
them. There can even be a collective emotional high which the
loving shepherd will feast on like a vampire on virgin's blood. You
may see it as part of your work actually to pull people down from
such a pitch of ecstasy, to a more everyday state, in which they are
ready to cope with the grumpiness and jeering of the rest of the
world. The group has been a part of their lives, no less and no more
than everything else they experience. One of many things they may
learn by the end of it, is more of what they want in life, and how to
aim for it.

EPITAPHS

*Here is an exercise to focus people back in their individual lives,
rather than only mourning the end of their collective one.
Ask everyone to shut their eyes and spend three minutes deciding
what they would like to see written on their gravestones when they
are dead. Ask them even to write these epitaphs. Then in pairs or
larger sub-groups let them talk about the epitaphs, and to tell each
other what they have done lately which is appropriate to what is
written. Finally they can tell each other what each person is going to
do in the next day or week which will be in line with their epitaph.*

CO-OPERATIVE LEARNING

When a group has had a short and apparently intense life, I like to do this exercise in its last hours. Again, ask people to pair, and take pen and paper. Send them off where they want to go, with a clear time for re-convening. The task is for them to take turns recalling what they have learnt in the group, formally or informally, about others and themselves, through their feelings as well as their heads. When A talks, B makes notes for her, and vice-versa. The talking aloud seems warmer than silent individual work, and triggers memories for both of them.

RITUALS OF ENDING

You can devise your own rituals in the group, to help you both express and contain some of what you are feeling at parting. We all need rituals. But, like clothes, rituals wear out and have to be replaced. Shaking hands and saying Well All The Best may still be appropriate for some of you, some of the time. For others it will be as unsatisfactory as hugging every single member - a group ritual which is quite common, and which sometimes looks to me a way of pretending that everyone's affection is at the same pitch to everyone else. Which is not often likely.

Saying Appreciations and Resentments; reporting what you have copied or remembered, what in short you have taken as a kind of present from other people; these are verbal rituals. Turning round in your circle so you are in contact, but facing out, and leaving when you are ready to, is a silent ritual of parting I have used. It may help you think of others to suit yourselves more exactly.

Make the ending you need to, and you acknowledge and underline more reality.

15. SUPERVISION - HELPING THE HELPERS.

If you are the designated leader in a group, then in one sense you are isolated: you are the only one of your kind in sight. Doing any job all alone leaves you without bench-marks. You need to see other people's standards, problems, habits, styles, and use their experience to enhance your own. So I recommend very strongly indeed that all small-group leaders meet others, for peer, or led, supervision time.

There are advantages to both kinds. But many institutions do not find the time or money for supervision, so you may decide to try peer supervision for cheapness as well as anything else.

Most of what I say here is aimed at peer supervision groups. I see more health in letting leadership be a function, be what-happens, than a role, a who. So if you experiment with working as a group of peer-leaders, you may later set up other groups which give more validation of the leader in every group member.

A supervision group is a species of Like Group. At worst it may be a florid sibling rivalry group.

Richard Beckhard calls this activity Measuring Cocks. All the statements in it add up to "Mine's better than yours". Everyone feels tense, knowing that if one person wins and has the Biggest or Best, everyone else has lost.

To change tack takes courage and honesty. Certainly, I am not over-fond of admitting to my peers that I am feeling dull and stupid in one of my groups, or that I have fallen into the elephant-pit carefully dug by a hostile group member. I don't want to seem the skill-less ignoramus. But I do want to deal with my anxieties, and hear other people freely do the same.

So the next caveat is against letting a peer group turn into an Ain't-it-Awful? session, with people capping each other's anecdotes of the ghastly moments they have lived through in their groups. One way to bust through to the useful aspect of an Ain't-it-Awful story is to focus on the speaker's role in what she is telling.

I think that one of many valid answers might be, "I just want to get rid of some of my irritation with this woman". If members stay aware of what they are talking for, they are self-monitoring, and are less likely to go into vertical take-off, lost in the content of their story.

A BAD SUPERVISION CONVERSATION
Well I wouldn't allow it in my group
O, you always get one or two like that.
Why not ignore her?
Have you tried...?

A GOOD SUPERVISION CONVERSATION
Since the first edition of this book appeared, I have written a whole book on Supervision and Counselling. That will give you

many more ideas, for different methods of supervision for different stages and kinds of work. Here is a potted supervision conversation. It shows a decently tough way of letting a member get to the core of her own difficulty, rather than be subjected to the "Well if I was in your shoes", or "Have-you-tried-X?" advisory approach, which can be very tempting, but is not always to the point.

S is the person being supervised, G is any other group member.

> S: Well I can't just tell her to be quiet.
> G: You can. It's possible.
> S: Well I don't want to.
> G: Why?
> S: It would be bad for her. Quite damaging.
> G: What are you saying about you?
> S: That I don't want to hurt people.
> G: What would happen if you hurt her?
> S: She might walk out.
> G: And what does that do to you?
> S: I'd feel terribly guilty. Powerless.
> G: Perls says that guilt is resentment turned back on

yourself.

> S: Well I certainly resent her.
> G: She makes you feel powerless? Sit on the chair and be

her. Pretend you're her, talking to you as the group-leader.

SUPERVISION ROLE-PLAY

Another way of working on S's problem member is to ask her to play the role of that member, while someone in the supervision group plays the role of S. People can take turns playing S. In the other role S. will find the effect of different interventions, at least on her, and from that may see other ways of approaching her problem person next week.

You may also gain insight from a more elaborate lead-in to this role-swapping. The person presenting a problem, Cecil, sets up the scene he is talking about, in this way. After a brief outline of what is bothering him, he goes and stands behind someone he would like to become a central character.

He puts his hands on, let us say, Janet's shoulders, and speaks as if he is the person Janet is to play. For instance:
"I am Rebecca. I am 50 and divorced and Jewish, and lost over 40 members of my family in the holocaust. I suppose I am terribly angry. But all I let out is a sort of dominating sweetness, and I talk and talk through every group session." Even doing this, Cecil is likely to make more empathic connection with Rebecca than if he talked about her in the third person. He places other people to play other significant characters, in his group or in Rebecca's life, as he sees fit. Then he casts someone to be himself.
"I am Cecil. Looking at Rebecca I feel rebellious, that I won't let her take over. Then I'm guilty for what she's been through." The person being enroled can ask information questions about the role, using the first person. Whoever is to play Cecil might ask "Do I see Rebecca as my mother in some way, and de-skill myself that way?"
When all are briefed, Cecil watches while the group enacts next week's meeting, or at least a few minutes of it. He has told what is not going right, and the ways people behave. They do their best to stay true to what they were instructed, while the new Cecil works to bring a fresh solution. If there is time, others can take Cecil's role, too. Then you all talk over what has happened and what Cecil has learned. He is likely to have taught himself a good deal.

A good deal of time is likely to be passed in such ways, in reviewing particular difficult moments for different members. As in any other group, you need to watch the balance, and check that you are not bewitching yourselves into noticing nothing but your difficulties. A round of telling moments you are proud of in your recent groups, could be the antidote.

As well as the important fine detail, some large questions are usefully dealt with in a supervision group.

What are people really about?

What am I really up to when I'm leading a group?

Questions as vast as this are bound to occur to you. Hearing other people's answers as well as your own can enlarge your view, and make you more assured.

You may be fortunate if you have people in your supervision group who work in different ways, from differing assumptions. You may also discover likenesses between our assumptions and ways of working, and understand more of each other's formal methods.

It looks to me as if it is just as hard for professional counsellors, therapists and group-leaders to broach the subject of what goes on between them, as it is for anyone else. In a peer or led supervision group, the out-there issues of your other groups may after a while become a very safe topic indeed. Yet there is a great deal to be learnt too from what is going on between you and in the supervision group. Who gets the most talking time? Who keeps being interrupted? Who becomes Joker, Worryguts, Little Professor? You are stacking up frustration, and missing a chance to learn, if you do not give some time to some of this right-here work.

One development from spending time on the here and now of the group, can be gradually to turn it into an inter-personal or counselling group. That may be what the members need. But they need supervision too. You need to think hard and openly about whether you want to combine the two.

All I have said assumes that you can find colleagues with whom to form a supervision group. For some workers this is not possible. So what do you do?

At the very least, I suggest you find a partner with whom you have a regular meeting, even a working lunch, with a clear agenda. Half the time the attention is with one of you and her work, half with the other. This, and an occasional day's or weekend's training to stimulate your ideas, maybe what you have to settle for in the short term.

As well as supervision outside your group, I see huge benefits for everyone concerned, in asking the group you lead to give a little time each week to monitoring you and themselves.

CHINESE SELF-CRITICISM

I know groups where there is a formal Chinese Self-Criticism half-hour at the end of each session, in which the task is to evaluate, rather than carp. The rule is that each person starts by focussing on evaluating their own part in what has been going on, rather than telling each other how they could have been more this or that.

As a leader who asks to be evaluated regularly, you challenge the members of your group to use their best judgement, and you are likely to hear some very insightful comment, from which you need to learn. As leader, too, you may at times need to listen carefully, to find whether people are avoiding the discomfort of confronting you, or taking the opportunity for vengeful onslaught.

This aspect of supervision, right at the coal-face, is very important indeed. It is a way of checking from session to session, on what everyone sees the group to be about, what they, and what you, expect you to be doing, and whether you are doing it effectively. I have often heard group-leaders explain that this is a fine idea, but that it would not be suitable for the groups they work with.

I have never yet found a group incapable of commenting on my work in a way I could learn from.
So, this form of supervision is always available, and I recommend, should always be used.

Outside supervision is very important too. One odd and good effect of the Treaty of Rome has been to concentrate people's minds, and even make them emulate the British Association for Counselling in requiring supervision throughout practitioners' careers. Treaty or not, you need monitoring, and encouraging, in what can be taxing and subtle, and at best very rewarding, work.

Gaie Houston first studied group behaviour with National Training Laboratories in the United States. She has worked as a consultant in many organisations, in many countries, is a UKCP registered psychotherapist, and is currently based with the Gestalt Centre, London, She has written a number of radio and theatre plays, and eight books on human behaviour. **The Red Book of Groups** and **Now Red Book of Gestalt** have been in print for over twenty years. Recently she has written **Brief Gestalt Therapy**, [Sage 2003] and, with Maja O'Brien, **Integrative Therapy** [Sage 2000].

*THE GROUP ALIVE
*THE RED BOOK OF GROUPS
*THE NOW RED BOOK OF GESTALT
*SUPERVISION AND COUNSELLING
*HERE AND NOW COOKERY, The Therapist in The Kitchen
INTEGRATIVE THERAPY, a Practitioner's Handbook
BRIEF GESTALT THERAPY

Full details of these books are on the web site www.gaiehouston.co.uk. They can all be obtained from bookshops or direct from

Gaie Houston, 8, Rochester Terrace, London NW1 9JN. UK

Starred books are available from this address post free within the UK.

THE RED BOOK OF GROUPS
Copyright Gaie Houston 1984 and 1990
2nd Revised Impression 1987
3rd Revised Edition 1990
4th Impression 1993
5th Impression 1998
6th Impression 2004.
Printed by M.F. Barnwell, Penfold St., Aylsham, Norfolk.
Cover design by Anne McArthur.
Published and distributed by The Rochester Foundation.

SWINDON COLLEGE

LEARNING RESOURCE CENTRE

INDEX OF EXERCISES